Facets & Fragments:
A Collage of Works from the Write On! Writers' Group

First Edition

Facets and Fragments:
A Collage of Works from the Write On! Writers' Group

Copyright ©2005

Write On! Writers' Group
P.O. Box 459
Los Gatos, CA 95031
wewriteon@yahoo.com

All rights reserved. No part of this book may be reproduced or transmitted in any form or by any means, electronic or mechanical, including photocopying, recording or by any information storage and retrieval system, without written permission from the authors, except for the inclusion of brief quotations in a review.

ISBN 0-9763318-1-0

Printed in the United States of America

Cover design by Jeff Brand

Acknowledgements

We thank Lara Owen for providing the spark that brought us together, and for inspiring and encouraging us.

Sincere thanks to Jeff Brand, who listened to our desires and designed the beautiful cover.

A special thank you to our photographer, Matt Mulbry.

We thank our proofreaders Kenneth Chastain, Mary J. Combs, Alex Crawford, Mary Gilliland, David Lazarony, Jr., Sharon Nelson, Rose Rappaport, Susan Rappaport, and Joan Valdes.

Contents

Acknowledgements. iii
Introduction / *Eileen McLaughlin*. 6
Dedication 9

Time, Place & Space
Watermelon / *Barbara Lazarony*. 12
Poem to My Little Black Cat / *Monique Mulbry*. 13
The Drive Home / *Eileen McLaughlin*. 15
Sit! Pocketbook / *Barbara Lazarony*. 17
Plastic Bag / *Eileen McLaughlin*. 18
What I Want / *Wendy Lewis*. 19
The Journey / *Wendy Lewis*. 21
Fear Rides on Two Wheels / *Betsy Gilliland*. 23
The Wind Chimes of Kriti / *Eileen McLaughlin*. 26
Stamping Out Corruption / *Betsy Gilliland*. 34

Coming of Age
Ode to Rainbow / *Barbara Lazarony*. 44
More / *Barbara Lazarony*. 45
Singing / *Wendy Lewis*. 46
Seven Names of Separation / *Barbara Lazarony*. 47
The Guidance Counselor / *Wendy Lewis*. 49
Miss You, Love You / *Traci Post*. 52
Memory / *Wendy Lewis*. 54
Questions / *Wendy Lewis*. 55
Bee Stings / *Monique Mulbry*. 57

Love & Lust
No Words / *Wendy Lewis*. 68
Angels in the Garden / *Traci Post*. 69
Two Step and Other Dances / *Monique Mulbry*. 72
Sex and Chocolate / *Liza Wood*. 94
Betrayal / *Wendy Lewis*. 101

Transitions
Black-Tie Optional / *Barbara Lazarony*. 104
Sawmill / *Barbara Lazarony*. 105
A Moment / *Eileen McLaughlin*. 106
Lighthouse / *Barbara Lazarony*. 107

Courage / *Wendy Lewis*. *109*
Cancer / *Wendy Lewis*. *110*
Recovery / *Wendy Lewis*. *111*
The Raft / *Wendy Lewis*. *113*
Fear / *Traci Post*. *115*
Sloe Dog / *Liza Wood*. *117*
Broken Windows, Empty Hallways / *Traci Post*. *124*
I Cry / *Eileen McLaughlin*. *133*

Living and Writing
The Backyard / *Barbara Lazarony*. *138*
Impressions of Uzbekistan / *Betsy Gilliland*. *140*
The Winter / *Wendy Lewis*. *142*
Turtle Faith / *Wendy Lewis*. *143*
Why I Write Poetry / *Barbara Lazarony*. *145*
In Silence / *Wendy Lewis*. *146*
Poetry is... / *Barbara Lazarony*. *147*
Wishing / *Betsy Gilliland*. *148*
Writer's Block / *Eileen McLaughlin*. *150*

The Authors
Betsy Gilliland. 152
Barbara Lazarony 153
Wendy Lewis. 154
Eileen McLaughlin 155
Monique Mulbry 156
Traci Post. 157
Liza Wood. 158

How to Contact Write On!. 159

Introduction
by Eileen McLaughlin

Courage. We all had it. One by one, we found our way to the classroom door, to a place to sit and lay down our writing pads, pens and stacks of collage-building materials. All we really had in common was the newly found courage to show up that day. We would expose our on-the-fly writing skills to a roomful of strangers. We would listen as others read their own creations and feel humbled by them. But we stayed and let the instructor make us believe that we, too, could turn ourselves into productive writers.

That was the beginning. From what might have otherwise been an unremarkable day in June 2001, the little writers' group we call *Write On!* formed and grew.

Surely, we had been attracted to that particular workshop for different reasons. All of us had done some writing before that day, but in different ways, drawing from different levels of study and skill. The workshop's description began by asking: "Have you wanted to write for months or years...?" In some way or another that query described us all. We came.

We have to give Liza full credit as our organizer. After all, she was the one who had already been in a writers' group. She knew the ropes. She volunteered to publish the contact list. She offered her home for the first meeting. Some people on the list never made it to any meeting. Five of us did and still do, though Liza's marriage and move make her an e-mail member now.

It didn't take us long to find our unifying bond among words that had followed us from the workshop. For minutes we sat, engrossed, listening to a reading of Mary Oliver's poem, "The Journey." Its words spoke to each of us and to all of us. Now and then, someone will mention the poem in our meetings. It hangs on Eileen's office wall. Its metaphor has made its way into Wendy's work. It is shared with friends who need it. It is a sustaining thread.

We've added a person now and then. Some tried joining us and didn't return. Traci and Barbara joined and stayed, each enriching and renewing Write On!. Some come occasionally. Some take life breaks. Some are regulars. While we have, over time, opened our meetings to a few men, we have settled into being an all-female affair. We usually meet at one another's homes, or sometimes at Borders Books.

We've chosen to think a bit independently about the rules of writers. "Write every day!" they say. Tipping our collective head to that wisdom, we had to allow room for our varied lives and time to conquer the obstacles of a writer's journey. We gave ourselves the right to personal point systems. Reading, reading about writing, writing for organizational newsletters, editing other writers, taking more writing classes, and attending plays all add up. There is no official record – just the sharing of it all in meetings and e-mail. It all seems okay. We're doing it our way.

As time has passed, some members have advanced to more regular writing routines, earning our admiration. Betsy was the first to be published. Hooray! Some of us published pieces in job-related and nonprofit media. Others ventured, hopefully, into the world of writing contests. Some began to lay their work before the eyes of more critical teachers.

Some members are not so brave or perhaps not so organized or perhaps just dealing with life's complications. That's okay. We are convinced: The day will come when we hear of the first writer's award among us.

It was Monique who initiated our book project. She saw that it was time to place our work before an audience, much like the recitals of musicians and dancers. She prompted us to again put courage before trepidation. Each of us, thus summoned, contributed from our individual places within the writer's process. The project inspired new works and timely rewrites. It pulled from deep within some old portfolios and from semi-professional publishing skills found among us.

We hope, dear reader, that you will read expectantly, awaiting the pleasure of small gems in our offerings. In this penned concert, we celebrate our varied journeys as writers and the unflagging support that we give to one another. We rejoice in the emerging truth of Mary Oliver's words in "The Journey":

> *the stars began to burn*
> *through the sheets of clouds,*
> *and there was a new voice*

We are most grateful that you join us in this celebration. You honor our courage in placing *Facets and Fragments* before you.
Courage begets courage.

We Write On!

Dedicated to all of our teachers and mentors, family and friends, and readers who have helped us along the way.

Time, Space & Place

Barbara Lazarony

Watermelon

Yank the curly-queue pig's tail free
Smash green waves across your hip
Gaze down at the watery pink fruit
Exposed

Bite letting the air escape
Swallow the sugar dripping down your throat
Wonder upon the mystery of its creation
Revealed

Spit black seeds into the ground
Mixing your saliva with its hope
Sowing a new life
Divine

Monique Mulbry

Poem to My Little Black Cat

Little black cat,
with the Mama who loves him
and the Papa who loves him.
In the little pink house
with the big back yard
and the brick walk way
that goes round-a-round.
And the birds
that sing-a-sing.

The neighbor, Art,
who lives next door
in the house
with the fish pond
to watch-a-watch.
And the shed
with the shady roof
to lounge on,
on lazy, hot days.

The dogs in the neighborhood
go bark-a-bark
as he tiptoes
along the fence line
to Harry and Faye's
for a cool, cool drink-a-drink
of water
from the fountain
that goes splash-a-splash.
And Harry's hand
that goes scratch-a-scratch
behind little black ears.

When night falls,
on the little pink house,
the crickets
go chirp-a-chirp.
And waiting at the door
is the Mama who loves him
and the Papa who loves him,
little black cat.

Eileen McLaughlin

The Drive Home

Doing the dance of the lanes,
the wheels beneath step across and between,
slowing, queuing after and before others,
positioning in the daily trip past
the electronic toll booth.

A beep, a flashed signal and another beep;
one more toll charged to the account.

Depressing the gas pedal,
commute auto-pilot kicks in:
practiced, strategic lane-merge maneuvers,
the end-of-the-day reversal that begins
on the bridge approach.

Flat spans of slough, salt pond and marsh
stretch north and south, levee-bound
and road-split, tarred pavement edging
the waterscape's silent, silvered-blue.

Pond-massed, reflection-doubled,
stilts and avocets present in black and white,
counterpoint to muted tans and browns
of sandpipers and muddy shore.

Meandering, the slough plays host
to a smattering of ducks, dabbling and diving;
fewer now than in days just past.

Westward headed in lane of habit,
eyes release the day's demands in ready

and eager trade for the boundlessness
of bay and sky.

A cloudless day is ending,
the sun is higher and winter is on the wane.

There, ahead and above,
the pale blue fills, unexpected and swift,
absorbing an illusory-gray swarm,
front-rounded and broad, soon thinning
to comet-like end.

Tantalized, road-conscience lapsed,
eyes feast, protesting even to blink.

The road lifts from land,
the swarm closer, easier to follow.
Specks emerge, hundreds alike,
wings in the motion of spring migration.
Tiny silhouettes move up and back
within the smooth, amoeba-like perimeter;
an unending dance repositioning,
reshaping the whole.

The mind flies free, merges with the flock
to wonder on its heading, its destination.

Just past mid-span and inevitably,
the road tilts downward,
the splendid free spirits disappear,
state of sight and mind return
to lane and traffic as the bridge reconnects
with the land.

The far shore's wetlands too quickly pass
and precede suburbia.

Sit! Pocketbook

Listening to the spiraling sounds...
the marketing gurus have been at it again,
I heard a commercial on the radio the other day.
The sad thing was that "thing" they were trying to sell me is lost.
I can't remember for the life of me what it was...
but the "image" stuck,
a woman had her handbag dyed and styled to match her dog.

You know, I know very little about dogs, but what if...
a woman carried a purse resembling a chocolate Labrador Retriever?
Or a man pulled a wallet out of his back pocket that talked like the "Taco Bell" Chihuahua?
Would we laugh?
Break a smile even?
Or should we call the Vet to have it spayed or neutered?
How about setting out a bowl of water for it on a hot sunny day?
Or do we just lean down and say,
"Oh what a beautiful pocketbook!"

Eileen McLaughlin

The Plastic Bag

Thin, light, leakproof,
easy.
Out somewhere,
picnic, game, fish.
Breeze,
billow, airborne.
Catch it?
Can't, didn't see.
Gone.

Beach, levee, marsh:
plastic-plastered,
encased.
Logo, retail, fastfood,
bubbled, bloated, anchored
in free space.

Bayside
hike, bike, at rest.
Helpful spirit.
Grab, yank, peel.
Oh, ugh, no, away.
Awful stench.
Sulfur, slime,
muck, brown, organic,
bag-bred
foul.

Wendy Lewis

What I Want

I think I'll know it when it arrives.
I'm not like other people,
who set a goal and go after it.
They take classes, get degrees,
save money.

Instead, I float,
so delicate,
like a flower petal
drifting on the water.
If a boat goes by,
the current changes my direction
and I swirl into eddies
and wash up on rocks and twigs.

I want to be an otter,
choosing my own direction
and gracefully sliding through
the water, doing flips and turns
along the way.

I'd like to swim so effortlessly
that I never lose my breath.
I don't want to reach the shore.

I think I'll know it when it arrives,
the feeling right and solid.
I remember watching an otter
at a zoo in Pittsburgh.

She swam fast and smooth
in figure eights to the end
of the pool and back,
never stopping.

She was strong and sleek.
But now I wonder if she loved
her pool or hated it.
Was she looking for an opening
as she followed its sides?
Or was she just enjoying the
fluid motion, weightless in water?

Did she yearn for the currents of a river,
Or was she happy
that the caretaker came
and threw fish to her
at the same time every day?

Wendy Lewis

The Journey

He said she was a shining star,
though only one among a million,
sparkling against the velvet sky.
Ordinary, but special anyway,
without trying.

She wanted a map to follow,
even one with torn edges
that didn't fold right any more.
Instead he gave her a silver compass,
and said, "Find your own way.
It's different than any other."

So she set off in the wrong direction,
tripping over her own feet.
She slept in the woods,
leaning against ancient tree trunks.
And sometimes bears and
coyotes followed her.

She bathed in cold streams
that rushed over rounded pebbles.
She warmed herself, naked
on smooth boulders,
heated by the day.

She wandered south, then west,
walking toward golden sunsets.
Sometimes plodding with heavy feet
and sometimes hopping over fallen
branches, barely touching ground.

And she knew she was a shining star
when she looked up and saw the
same night sky every time.

And she was no longer hungry
for food or touch.
The bed she made was soft with
green moss. It smelled fresh,
like newly turned earth
warmed in afternoon sun.

And then it was his turn to ask her
for answers. And she held the secrets
close between them,
and whispered her directions
to make him feel safe.

Betsy Gilliland

Fear Rides on Two Wheels

My parents raised their children with the confidence that we knew right from wrong and safe from dangerous. They never lectured us directly about motorcycles, but instead operated on the assumption that we had enough common sense to avoid these death traps on wheels. One day when I was about ten, we encountered an accident in which a motorcycle had flipped. The rider lay on the asphalt, his face writhing in pain, his leg and his arms broken, blood gushing from acute lacerations all over his body. He wasn't wearing a helmet, and my mother clucked about how lucky he was to still be alive. That day, I swore never to ride a motorcycle. Ever.

Fast forward twenty years to the countryside near Ayuthaya, Thailand, my friend Cristin and myself standing by the side of an interstate highway as cars and trucks rush by at 70 miles an hour. Dropped off by a Bangkok-bound bus that unbeknownst to us did not go all the way to the bus station in the center of Ayuthaya, we were stranded. Strangely for Thailand, not a single person on our bus spoke English, and the conductor insisted through gestures and tone of voice that we disembark, dragging us off by the wrists and tossing our luggage after us. Since we'd only paid to go this far, there was no reason to let us stay on her bus. She did not care what became of us once we were no longer her passengers.

The bus pulled back onto the road and motored away into the distance. Shocked, we stood watching the traffic and pondering how we had wound up in the dark by a highway with no city in sight, wondering how we would get to our destination.

Two wiry young men on motorcycles approached us from the far side of the median and asked if we wanted a taxi. A wave of relief washed over me. A taxi! We were saved. A taxi at any price could take us into the city and drop us at our hotel.

"Yes!" we both cried. "Where is the taxi?"

The men pointed at the pale blue vests they both wore over their short-sleeve cotton shirts. My heart sank as I read "TAXI" written in large white English letters. Motorcycles are much more common vehicles on Thai highways than they are in the United States. Thai motorbike owners can become licensed as taxi drivers, carrying passengers on the back of their scooters.

"Are you the taxi?" They nodded yes. "We want a car taxi. Where is a car taxi?"

"No car. Just motorbike taxi."

I swallowed the fear rising in my throat. I did not want to ride a motorbike taxi. I could see from her grimace that Cristin did not either. "Will you get us a car taxi?" she asked one of the motorbike men.

"No. It is dark. No car taxis come here at night."

"Then how do we go to Ayuthaya?"

"50 baht. You ride on my motorbike."

My knees grew weak as I thought of the man lying on the pavement twenty years earlier. I thought of all the things I hadn't done yet in my life, the places I hadn't been, and the people I hadn't met. Then I thought of all the people I had met and how they would feel when they heard I had died on a rural Thai highway, my neck broken, my blood pouring out like water from a tap. I didn't want to cause my friends and family that kind of pain.

Then I started to weigh our options. If we didn't take the motorcycle taxi to the center of Ayuthaya, I didn't know what we would do that evening. It was clear from the bare grass and trees that there weren't any hotels by the highway. There weren't even any other roads beyond the highway. We couldn't speak or read Thai. We didn't know where we were nor how to get to Ayuthaya. We had no food to eat nor weapons to protect ourselves from roadside bandits. If we didn't take the motorbike taxi, it appeared that we'd stand as much of a chance of dying as if we did take the taxi. At least the motorbike drivers claimed to know where Ayuthaya was.

I saw Cristin mulling over these same concerns. We looked

at each other, sighed, and agreed to the taxi ride. We shouldered our backpacks and each straddled a motorcycle behind the drivers. They had helmets. We didn't. Before I could think of anything to say to Cristin in farewell, our drivers revved their motors and zipped out onto the highway. The bikes leaned precariously going around corners. I gripped my driver's waist and hoped I was not making a cultural faux-pas that would inspire him to push me off the bike in the middle of the road.

The cool wind on my face and the sounds flying by so enthralled me that I momentarily forgot my fear. First the smell of fresh country grass, then the chemical odors of city life blew into my nostrils. The dark night gave way to neon lights. Honking horns and blaring pop music streamed through my ears. Adrenaline pumped through my veins.

Even long after we had gotten off the bikes and paid the drivers, my heart beat a little faster and my eyes blinked a few more times than necessary. My legs shook from the rush. We were still alive, and we were standing in front of the hotel, in the center of Ayuthaya.

Cristin says she spent the entire twenty-minute ride praying, something she doesn't ordinarily do. Maybe I should have prayed, too, but at the time I was so caught up in the moment that I could think of nothing but the wind and the lights. I'm still afraid of motorcycles, but now I feel more justified in my fears–I know what it is like to ride one. I haven't yet told my parents about the ride.

Eileen McLaughlin

Wind Chimes of Kriti

Time transient,
cherished moments collect in memory and soul.
Events, places, links of person and person,
elusive, exclusive energies imbued on unique occasions,
reaching the innermost core of spirit.
Forever they nourish the soul.

Klank, klack, klink....

Perhaps the Kriti visit came at a time of senses
acutely open, mind and spirit exquisitely permeable,
receptive as dry sponge to water.
Midway, the land had me wholly captured,
senses, mind and soul enveloped,
diffused into each and every cell and space
within my physical self.
It had my heart. It became one with my spirit.

Klunk, klink, klack, klack....

By choice and whim and transport,
half a world was I from country and culture and origin.
Now as foreigner, there to wander, to wonder.
A day on a mountainside, an outlook on the Libyan Sea,
my self and soul thus and there overwhelmed,
every sense engaged, vibrant.
Days prior became one with that day;
days after, nurtured, enriched,
embedding it all, deeper, deeper.

    Klink klink klunk klack klank
    Klunk klackety klunk

Wind Chimes of Kriti / *Eileen McLaughlin*

Klink klink klack klunk klunk

Solo and duo,
trio and orchestra,
harmony in complement and competition.

Notes strung together
irregular and overlapping,
de facto as composition and celebration,
underscoring voices
of the katsiká.

Every note freeform and voice unexpected.
So were the wind chimes of Kriti.

Klink klink klunk klack klank
Klunk klackety klunk
Klink klink klack klunk klunk

The wind had changed our plans,
had created a new plan and a new day.
It was that wind and the hillside music evoked,
that would reach deep within.
Tonal vibrations would instantly link
so many sensations already consumed.

Klink, klack, klank...

Stopped at a switchback in the trail,
we soon would continue each zig and zag
of a long, steep descent.
Moments to reflect on the panorama we stood within.
Yes, within.

Earlier, an absolutely extraordinary panorama had lain
fully before us, from the mountain's crest,
on the grounds of the small Chapel of St. Catherine.
Enormous vistas of sky, land and sea
drew the senses outward then deeply inward.
Feeling very small and gifted and humble,

it was so very right that a chapel was placed just there.
Again, another tiny, well-tended,
white-washed Greek Orthodox chapel,
found everywhere and anywhere,
often, starkly, symbolically alone.
Piety and tradition, art and nature and daily life
were as one.

East and west of us the steeply sloped coast
met the gorgeous blues of the Libyan Sea,
spanning the entire horizon.
Far away, all across the southern reach of our vision,
gray mists lay where the waters met the sky.
A pair of darkened outlines, barely perceptible,
ghostly silhouettes,
the most southerly islands of Greece.
The larger of them is said to be Calypso,
the island storied in ancient Greek myths.
Belief validated as truth
by mist-shrouded, spectral visage.

Klack, klunk klink, klunk...

Striking white buildings, below us,
captive within a peninsula's curve.
Our destination, the tiny town of Loutro,
idyllic, even from afar.
Rocky cliffs surround, tower above the small bay,
orange and brown in rock and earth,
sprinkles of greenery barely seen.
Waters richly blue, too distant yet
to sense their tides, their rhythms.
Glistening buildings fill, grace, a narrow, spare shore.
The cliffs sharply rise and more structures cling,
paint-dressed, bright blue upon white.
From skyward vantage, vertical layers of human presence
framed by water and rock.

A few boats lay moored,
simple in shape, small, white,

as on display in the rich blue of the bay.
The ferry, white too, larger,
floating pier-side, that day hobbled by the winds.
Trail and boat, the only ways
to or from Loutro.
Oh so splendid the isolation.

Jutting into the sea,
the plateau'd peninsula bore mankind's traces.
Oh yes, there again, a white chapel
perched at one edge, water beyond.
Inward from the sea, forms and shadows of ancient Kriti
blended, toned in gray and brown.
A thick-walled, ancient cylinder rises,
still solid, standing alone.
Elsewhere, walls grouped, once squared and roofed,
now ragged, broken, open to the sky.
Venetian and Turkish reminders survive,
side by side.
Unseen yet and camouflaged by distance,
stones of field wall and hut, arches,
some in place, scattered, re-used,
telling of the Roman presence there, too.
Layers of time, century upon century past.

Not for the first time, but again,
a sense pervasive,
the persistence of antiquity everywhere.
On this island and in this part...of our world.

New world roots feeling in stark contrast,
as in youthful simplicity.
Pride and patriotism mitigated.
Millennia ago, it is true,
ice sheets advanced and retreated
while peoples thrived on the "new"continent.
Neither scientist nor historian can there report
or reveal culture so old, so rich, so immense.
For humankind, the Mediterranean incubated,
Kriti fully encircled and involved,

civilizations rising and expiring,
again and again.

Ruins below, on days just before and still to come,
evoke awe beyond expression.
Barely, just barely,
can thought and spirit link reality of now to then.
So fragile a connection,
so few, so short the days to absorb.
Antiquity evident at every turn.
Cretans so enriched, day by day
by generations unending.

Klank, klink, klink, klinkety klunk....

Though May, it was cool, comfortable,
a hiker's gift as the winds swept the coast.
Clouds, small and few, moved swiftly,
rarely shadowing our trek nor interrupting
perspectives presenting all around.

Earlier and higher,
a griffon vulture glided, afloat, above the slope,
the breezes its ally.
Two and three thousand feet and more above the sea,
it was the vulture's domain.
Unique to this continent,
always above Greek mountains and gorges,
here, familiar, the common vulture.
Large, broad of wing,
white head upon a long neck,
downwardly curved beak.
Close enough were we to revel
in a birdwatcher's analogy in some year past,
anointing it with the mythical name of griffon.
Nature and antiquity connected.

Thus it was that my head whirled.
So many impressions.

Klank, klunk, klack, klink....

I stood briefly alone.
Now mid-slope, looking outward,
from deep within the panorama,
up toward the crest and white chapel and sky.
To the east and west,
up, down, across the great expanse of sloping mountains,
then to the sweep of sea from coast to horizon
and to the murk beyond.
Sensation upon sensation came together,
collided and united,
held within, enveloped by a landscape.
So simple. So much.
So hard to explain.

Then it was that I became aware of chimes,
airborne reminders of the land underfoot,
the slopes where we were not alone.
Amid the earth and rocks
and thorny burnet and poison onion,
we walked lands used by shepherds
for eons long past and yet still today.
Rock and ridge and slope,
what other place for foraging goats?

Tones in varied abundance,
wind ringing the bells of a meandering flock.
Simple, uncomplicated sounds,
the only music that belonged there.
Even to say–katsiká–was to hear rhythm
in the Grecian name for goats.
Goat to goat, each bell differs,
size, shape and metal,
with time, battered, bent,
tonality changed, exquisitely unique.

Roaming free, the goats easily amble, scramble

across, up and down rocky hillsides,
terrain that so challenged,
tested my every step.
With every move, each clapper
strikes yet again and then again
emitting its own klunk, klack, klank, or klink.

As the goats paused to graze or gaze at us,
the bells swayed with the wind alone
and seemed never silent.
The orchestra of bells chimed
in complement and in clash and in random repeat.
Voices of goats the chorus,
bleating heard every now, then, here, there.
Sounds harsh, nasal and abrupt,
in contrast to the ringing chimes.

Raw and real and beautiful,
overwhelming and extraordinary.
So very there was I.

As when an orchestra reaches dramatic crescendo,
the music of that moment and that place
carried abundant and immense sensations
into and through all
of my mind, my soul, my body.
In an instant, I was immersed, saturated,
every sense heightened.
My spirit soared and silently sang.

>   Klink klink klunk klack klank
>   Klunk klackety klunk
>   Klink klink klack klunk klunk

>   Solo and duo,
>   trio and orchestra,
>   harmony in complement and competition.

>   Notes strung together
>   irregular and overlapping,

de facto as composition and celebration.
Underscoring voices
of the katsiká.

Every note freeform and voice unexpected.
So were the wind chimes of Kriti.

Klink klink klunk klack klank
Klunk klackety klunk
Klink klink klack klunk klunk

Home, once again immersed in the familiar.
Wind chimes of wood, metal and clay
hang just outside, below the eaves.
Windows open for summer breezes,
I hear their gentle chimes,
a sensation now changed.

Forever, I think,
those chimes will send my heart racing,
back to that day, that hillside,
to the moment Kriti so completely filled me.
Again and again, I will feel unending joy.

Stamping Out Corruption

I was still in a good mood when we stopped for lunch at a ramshackle café perched on the darker side of a canyon. Downhill, below the road, an icy river trickled past shacks and rocky pastures. A rickety outhouse clung to the side of the hill above the café. We shivered under the thin sunlight, nibbling our bread and cheese sandwiches. After lunch, our entourage reconvened at the mini-bus. We squeezed back in, and the bus crawled onto the deserted highway through darker, steeper, rockier and less-inhabited valleys until finally we reached the barbed wire of the international border.

International borders did not often scare me. I was neither extremely poor nor outlandishly wealthy. I didn't look like a drug smuggler or a refugee. But stories I had heard about corruption among customs officials in the country I was entering plagued me the closer we got to the border.

I am not a hard-core adventure traveler. Insects disgust me, and I have no desire to put my life at risk in a war zone. I do, however, believe in taking advantage of an opportunity–hence my appearance on a mini-bus winding across the Caucasus Mountains at the end of October, accompanied by a fellow Peace Corps volunteer and nearly a dozen Armenian and Georgian business people. My Iran-born and New York-raised friend Shahram and I were en route from Yerevan, Armenia, to Tbilisi, Georgia, on the second leg of a comprehensive tour around the nations which had once formed the Southern boundary of the Soviet Union. We had arranged to stay in Tbilisi with my college friend who worked at the U.S. embassy. Because Shahram spoke no Russian, he often deferred to my knowledge of the language to translate our needs as we journeyed through the region. I relied just as often on his ability to read people without knowing a common language.

~~~

The primary highway between Armenia and Georgia, used by trucks pulling semi trailers and buses carrying full loads of passengers, must diverge far off the direct path in order to avoid the steepest of mountains. Only private cars and mini-buses can negotiate the hairpin turns and deep ruts of the shorter route. Some travelers drove their decades-old rusted Lada sedans and others hitched rides in newer Volvos, but most relied on the well-broken-in 10-passenger Toyota vans driven by entrepreneurs from both sides of the border. According to our Armenian hosts, who drove us to the Yerevan bus station and helped us find a ride, these vehicles could cross the border and arrive at their destination in half the time of the conventional bus.

The other passengers, all Georgians and Armenians, stared vacantly ahead, hardly acknowledging each other. A few briefcases and purses, their only luggage, fit neatly on their laps. We sat on the second of the three bench seats in the van, Shahram by the window on my left and me in the middle, next to a matronly dark-haired woman in a black wool coat and floral headscarf. Behind us two younger women in high-heeled black boots gossiped animatedly in Georgian. An older man in a thick fur hat took the front passenger seat opposite the driver, an Armenian with a lengthy nose and thick dark eyebrows. In our jeans and bright-colored coats, Shahram and I felt distinctly out of place as we stowed our monstrous backpacks, whispered cautiously in English, and gawked at the majestic natural scenery. Certainly we would be the obvious choice of any customs officer thirsting for trouble.

Late in the morning, we encountered some snow as we passed dry fields and bare trees in the rolling hills and sparsely populated countryside. The road produced more curves, pot-holes and cliffs than I had expected, but overall the ride itself was comfortable. The driver pulled over at the roadside café for lunch just as I thought I'd have to dig out my sandwich and disturb my neighbors by eating uncouthly in the bus. After lunch, I wasn't certain whether the knots I felt in my stomach were from the increasingly twisty road or my knowledge that the Georgian border would have to come soon.

Friends had warned us it would be almost impossible to get across the border without paying extra bribes to corrupt officials, but we were determined not to give in quickly. Even a reduced bribe would seem like a small victory over corruption.

~~~

Suddenly, a chain-link gate materialized in the otherwise uninhabited mountains. A faded red, blue and gold Armenian flag fluttered on a pole above the compound. A shivering Armenian soldier, khaki cap pulled down over his ears, guarded the gate. He glanced without interest into the van as our driver collected everyone's passport and strolled confidently into the Armenian customs house, in reality a building not much more than a hut. Within fifteen minutes he was back, passing the entire pile of newly-stamped passports to the woman sitting in the first row. She took hers and stoically handed the rest to her neighbor.

The driver put the bus in gear and drove slowly through the gate opened by the bored soldier. Having left Armenia, we stopped fifty yards ahead at the next gate, the entrance to Georgia. Another soldier, eyelids and cigarette drooping, guarded the gate. Another hut, smoke puffing out of the chimney, sat next to this fence. The only difference was the color of the flag–maroon, with white and black in the upper corner.

The driver collected our passports again and headed into the hut. After fifteen minutes, when he still hadn't returned, the men got out of the van to smoke. We foreigners followed, eager to stretch our legs after several hours of sitting. The air was crisp, the sky gray.

No-man's-land more resembled an abandoned logging camp than an international border. The fence extended only five feet beyond the sides of the road. A half-dozen wooden shacks clustered between the gravel and the hillside. On one side of the road, a steep hill sloped upwards into the rocky, tree-filled Caucasus mountains. On the other side, a grassy slope descended into a small valley. The soldiers had set up a volleyball net there. I wondered if they arranged international matches for entertainment, the Georgians against the Armenians.

Beyond the border post, there was no sign of life. The huts looked flimsy and uninsulated, just a few rooms where the customs officers sat and the soldiers warmed up from the cold around wood-burning stoves. The skinny young soldiers, armed with machine guns, slouched at the gate, smoking cigarettes and waiting for another car to appear.

~~~

Our fellow passengers were called into the Georgian customs office one by one. They returned as grim and silent as they had been on the ride so far. We had left Armenia in a matter of minutes, but we waited more than an hour to enter Georgia.

After most of our group had returned, the driver motioned for Shahram and myself to enter the customs hut. The previous passenger, a heavily made-up woman, was still there, so we waited awkwardly at the door. She sat on the officer's desk and slid her miniskirt higher up her leg while joking with him about visiting that night for drinks, her mannerisms suggesting she would pay her bribe in another currency. With one last giggle and a promise of more later, she skipped out of the hut.

We were alone with the Georgian customs officer, who held our passports in front of him. He surveyed us from under the brim of his oversized military cap, then directed us to sit and immediately began speaking to Shahram in Russian. "What is your purpose in visiting Georgia?" Shahram stared blankly at him.

I replied, "We're going to Tbilisi, to visit my friend."

"Can't your friend talk?" the officer asked me.

"He doesn't know Russian. I can translate for him."

The officer turned away from me and again addressed Shahram. He did not look at me for the rest of the interview.

"Where are you from?"

Shahram continued to gaze vacantly at the officer, who was running his fingers over our American passports. I again answered for both of us, "The United States."

He looked at Shahram. "Where are you coming from?"

"Yerevan," I snapped, irritated with his obstinate refusal to deal directly with me.

"Why do you want to go to Georgia?" Shahram blinked at him but remained mute.

"We want to visit all the countries in the former Soviet Union. We have been working in Uzbekistan and would like to learn more about this region."

The officer half-turned his head toward me, but continued to speak to Shahram. "Why do you want to go to Georgia?" he repeated, emphasizing the name of the country.

"Georgian wine is famous all over the world. Even in America we hear that Georgian people are known for their food and hospitality," I lied. "We would like to experience this for ourselves." I was pleased that I had remembered the Russian word for *hospitality*, though the customs official was not impressed.

He seemed satisfied with this answer, however, but he still did not turn over our passports.

He opened a drawer and pulled out a pile of small papers, about two inches square, which from my vantage point were blank.

"You must pay $20 each for this paper," he told Shahram.

I gestured at our passports. "But we already have visas. Look, we paid for them in Tashkent."

"Yes, but you don't have this paper. When you pay for it, I will put it in your passports."

"Why do we need that paper?"

"It's important. You won't be allowed to leave Georgia if you don't have this paper."

"We weren't told about that at your embassy. We won't

pay any more."

There was a long pause as he considered his next move. Looking pointedly at us, he opened a drawer and put the papers back in it. It slammed shut with a finality I had never before heard in cheap office furniture.

He then fingered the two rubber stamps on an ink pad at the left side of his desk. "I have two stamps here. You need both of them to go to Tbilisi, or you'll have trouble with the police there."

"Fine, stamp our passports so we can leave you to your work," I answered.

He rubbed his fingers over the stamps, almost caressing them in his fondness for the bureaucracy they represented. "You need to pay for the stamps. I can't give them to you for free."

We sat in silence for ten minutes that seemed an eternity. The wood stove crackled, releasing smoke but little heat into the room. A mustachioed officer tiptoed into the room to warm his hands over the stove and check out our passports, which he handed to another visiting soldier, who also admired them before returning them to the desk.

Our inquisitor eyed his beloved stamps, then looked at us again. "You do realize, don't you, that without that form the police could arrest you, and you will not be able to continue your trip."

"My friend works at the American embassy in Tbilisi. If there is a problem, she will help us."

"Your friend can't give you this form or this stamp. Only I can give you the stamp."

"I think the ambassador will help us if we have trouble."

Another pause. I had thrown a wrench in his routine, and he needed to contemplate thoroughly his next step. As we waited, the wood stove snapped and popped. I feared our bus would abandon us on the mountaintop, stuck in no-man's-land, where in desperation we would have to pay an even bigger bribe to escape.

With a sigh, our adversary magniloquently grasped one of his stamps, thumped it into the ink, then pounded it onto one passport. He looked up at us momentously as he forcefully re-inked the stamp, then repeated the show with the other passport. The task completed, he waved the passports in the air to dry the ink, set them back on the desk, and pushed them halfway across to us but did not remove his hand.

"I've given you one stamp. You may go now. But remember, you have only one stamp. You will have trouble leaving Georgia without the other one. Your embassy won't be able to help you." He turned away dramatically, gesturing with a flick of his wrist that we were to leave his presence immediately.

Saying nothing to each other, Shahram and I scurried back to the waiting mini-bus, which pulled away from the customs station the instant we had scrambled on board. I was trembling with anger and fear, my bravado from moments earlier melted in our release from the customs hut. I wondered if my fellow passengers could see my shaking hands as I repacked my passport. They didn't look at us, although I was sure they wondered how much bribe money the Georgian officer had exacted from us.

~

Shahram leaned against the window, his eyes glazed over, and he seemed to be deep in thought. Not wanting to draw attention to myself, I didn't say anything to him. I stared blankly at the trees, rocks and ancient mountain villages, my mind exhausted from the encounter. I dreaded each police checkpoint our bus approached, although no police asked to see our passports, demanded money for our missing stamp or even acknowledged our presence on the bus.

Dusk was falling as we approached Tbilisi. Each broken lamp post and crumbling brick wall announced that we had crossed the border and arrived at our destination, wallets unscathed. Never before had a decaying city appeared so welcoming.

Stumbling out of the bus, I glanced around nervously for police officers lurking in the shadows, still convinced I might be penalized for my missing stamp. Shahram stretched his arms, shaking off the lethargy of his eight-hour meditation. His eyes now clear, he turned to me and said, "I just realized that his second stamp was the exit stamp. No one entering the country ever gets that stamp—he can only give that when you leave!" My backpack suddenly felt much lighter, and we burst out laughing. With renewed confidence, we flagged down a taxi to go to my friend's house.

The Georgian wine at dinner that night tasted uncommonly rich.

Coming of Age

Barbara Lazarony

Ode to Rainbow, My Pig

I still remember the day we picked you up,
you rode at my feet in the feed bag on the pickup floor,
squealing at the loss of your Mother.
My Father smiled at me as we drove out the lane.

Through mud holes and bug swarms
we pushed forward,
out to the road,
to civilization.

You looked up at me the whole time,
you trusted me, I think.
Maybe I was to be your protector,
your confidant,
your salvation,
from a life that your Mother knew
and had only just begun to explain to you,
her blessed one.

But I was 12, and had a different goal for you, beloved.
A plan that my Father was in the process of teaching me,

> a lesson that runs so deep,
> that it is buried in my brain even today.

The Value of the Almighty Dollar:
1) Means so much to those who yearn for it;
the taste of sweet sunlight on your tongue.
2) Means so little to those who already know;
the beauty of raindrops caught in a beam
of light.

Barbara Lazarony

More

Give me more days...

holding hands,
whispering rain secrets,
skinning knees,
being afraid of long shadows,
giggling,
holding my new baby brother,
dressing Barbies,
catching lightening bugs,
folding down white socks,
being a little girl.

Wendy Lewis

Singing

In the back seat of the car,
squeezed between elbows and cousins,
her face turns hot.

"You are ruining the song,"
her aunt declares.
She thought that singing
meant opening her heart
and making a joyful noise.

Now she knows that she is wrong.
Hers doesn't come out right.
It is flawed.
Clear evidence that she is
wrong and bad,
a misfit who better keep quiet.

She'll squelch the voice inside
so no one else will know
that she can't follow a proper tune.

In the back seat of the car,
cheek pressed against the coolness
of the window, she hums quietly
to herself, her voice masked
by the vibration of the engine.

Barbara Lazarony

Seven Names of Separation

"She is acutely aware of her own strength, she knows, and still she knows...."

No longer a child,
my *Barbie* locks removed with shears
and a razor blade in Grandma's skilled fingers;
fumbling towards sadness and stillness at my loss.
I have a genetic pre-disposition to colors.

A *Barb* emerges to family and school children,
a straight smile, a sideways tilted head;
but bright eyed.
I like yellow.

A *BLY* appears on a scoop necked t-shirt with iron-on letters,
accentuating the pulse of lips and developing breasts; boys notice.
I like rainbow colors, especially warm and sunny orange.

A music teacher in ecstasy with the song of "Sin de Vel a ba"
and hysterical with the clinker sound of *Barb Young;*
attempting to fit in in the teenage years, how utterly impossible.
I hold yellow close, while wishing on a rainbow, but feeling really blue.

A realization of worldly interests gives birth to a *Barbara*,
calm, cool, a gentle lady on the outside;
a ball of string on the inside;
trying not to unravel the mystery while swallowing hard on cotton fiber.

I remember yellow hair on my favorite dolly and her
blue-black patent leather shoes.
I'm determined to embrace red.

A new friend, a new larger than life figure, coins a *Babs*,
it works for her, and eager to please, I follow blindly;
all the time remembering one who lives by the clickety clack
of railroad tracks
and sleeps with boys wanting to become men.
I like red, I think–but she said I need to like purple, her color.
I pretend to know purple, I still like red.

An illness, an insightful stillness ensues,
toweling the last drop of water off a body that questions if
it is friend or foe.
A *Blaz* emerges, still unaware, but confident and
more relaxed,
just my asking is important, for once I didn't pretend
to be the expert.
I walk into life's next adventure, eager
my head tilted a little to the right,
aware of my womanhood beneath my clothes,
the music of my voice,
and the sureness of my footing,
a wise student of life.
I like peach, a flesh tone;
a good sister to orange and yellow, a daughter of red,
a friend of purple, a distant cousin of blue.

Wendy Lewis

The Guidance Counselor

Why now, at age 51,
do I remember sitting in a stuffy office
with the grade school guidance counselor?

She asked me what I thought were my strengths,
and then the hard question,
what were the worst things about me.

I immediately thought,
"I'm lazy; I don't try hard enough."
I felt a guilty tingling in my arms,
and sweat forming across the base of my neck.
I knew that I couldn't tell this truth,
and that I probably couldn't talk without crying.
So I held my breath and felt my heart
beating hard in my thin little chest.

I challenged myself to just say it.
Why not? If I could just get it out
without my voice quavering,
it might be okay.
At least I knew the answer.

But she moved on to an easier question
and another about favorite subjects
and suddenly she snapped her notebook shut
and I realized the meeting was over.

My breath came back with relief
and disappointment.
I wanted to answer,

to confess my sins and be absolved
like the Catholic kids did.

And now, with the knowledge
that comes with middle age,
I wonder why she didn't wait a little longer.
I wonder why she didn't say,
"I won't tell anybody."
"It's okay to say what you are thinking."
"It's okay to cry."

Couldn't she see the pain
in my eight-year-old brown eyes?
Didn't she see my chapped lip trembling?
But I probably looked away,
and I was used to not being seen.
And maybe she didn't know what to do,
because there was a hurt and lonely girl
inside of her too,
and Eisenhower was still the president
and we didn't talk about that kind of thing anyway.

We didn't talk about homes where anger shook the floor
and crashed against the walls like a tidal wave
that churned around us so that we felt dizzy
and stopped knowing which way was up.

And I thought that if I just tried harder,
and washed myself more,
and didn't touch myself in bed at night,
if I just could figure out what they really wanted,
if I was quiet and good and didn't ask for anything,
I knew they would be happier.

If I just wasn't so lazy,
I knew I could make it right.
I could make them proud of me
and happy and maybe they'd hug me
and tell me I was good,
and not just to clean up my room and

don't you have any homework?
Stop chewing your hair,
and I'll give you something to cry about.

Now, at age 51, I want to hold the little girl
and tell her that it will be okay.
I want to tell her that it's good to cry if you are sad,
and that she is safe and loved.
I want to take her in my arms,
and rock her gently
and tell her she is good,
and special and smart
and that it's okay to be sad and angry sometimes.
I'd like to tell her that it's okay to make a mess,
because I'll help her clean it up.
I'd like to tell her that there is enough time
to take things slowly,
and sometimes you have to try
even if you don't think you can do it,
and sometimes you have to just trust for no good reason.
Now, at age 51, I would make her feel safe.

Miss You, Love You

Miss you.
Love you.
I say the words
wishing to hear little voices in return.

Miss you.
Love you.
Thanks for all that you do.
You brighten my days
crazy talk and mood swings, too.
Miss you. Love you.

Can't bridge the distance between our two hearts,
but the spirit of souls connects
through the space separating our bodies.
Miss you. Love you.
Can't wait to see you soon.

Please come home healthy.
Please come home happy–happy to see us.
You're our children, yet you are not.
Miss you. Love you.
Wish we could be there
experiencing your new discoveries.

Time is flowing quickly away,
soon you'll be grown and on your own.
Miss you. Love you.

Watched the sunrise this morning.
New blessed day dawned to the blackbird's song,
ushered in on nature's breath rustling the cherry tree.
Our arms won't hug and our voices won't touch,
not this sunny day anyway.
Miss you. Love you.
Can't wait to see you.

Wendy Lewis

Memory

I remember the stifling thickness of the air
when I came into the house after
running outside in the coolness of the evening.
Neighborhood games with my sister,
who always got chosen first when
the boys picked teams.

It is a different color than the memories
of more recent years–soft and dusky.
Gentle.

My mother's youngest brother died on Sunday,
and today, she told me that she called her
childhood friend (a rare occasion) and
learned she had died one month ago.

Oh for the soft and dusky times.

I hated my uncle, who never looked me in
the eye and punished his children harshly.
But I heard they were all there, by his
bedside when he died. All six boys.

And maybe I judged him too harshly with
the same anger that wanted the air
in the house to have the same freshness
as the inevitable approaching night.

Wendy Lewis

Questions

When I was only eight or nine,
I thought about the universe
and wondered what was at the end of it.

If you just went straight out into the sky,
I reasoned, eventually you would have to
come to something.

Like a wall, I thought.

But what was on the other side of that?
It frustrated me so much
that I had to force myself to stop thinking.
It made me angry, it made me crazy,
I worried.

My mother said there was a theory
that maybe you would come back
to where you started from.
Infinity.

But I thought maybe we were just
tiny microorganisms in a giant's fish tank.
But what was at the end of the giant's universe?
That really bugged me.

And I thought about an image in a mirror,
reflected in another mirror and it made me mad to
think of how many pictures within a picture
there really would be.

So now, I accept that these questions
cannot be answered.
But others bug me more.
Does life get better or worse?
Why do people have to suffer?
Is there any meaning to life, and if not,
why not?

To me, the question of infinity and
what comes after the stars is far less
important than questions like:
How can I help my sister's pain?
Why should I get out of bed?
And who should I love?

Is there a theory about these questions?
Perhaps I'll put them in the giant's fish tank
and come back to them at the beginning.

Monique Mulbry

Bee Stings

When Clara was really little, about five years old to be exact, she thought the worst thing God could send her way was a bee sting to the big toe. That was before her father died, leaving her and her mother alone in the Princeton Place house.

It was August, and Becca McBride, Clara's best friend, wanted to jump through her sprinkler to cool off. At seven, Clara thought she was too old to jump through sprinklers, but it was hot and the idea of icy water cooling her body sounded good, so Clara had agreed. She changed quickly into her purple and hot pink bathing suit, grabbed her Tom and Jerry beach towel and ran out of the house, skipping up the lawns of Princeton Place, toward Becca's.

When the McBrides first moved into the neighborhood, Mrs. McBride had marched down to Clara's house, Becca in tow, and knocked on their door. Mrs. McBride looked like Twiggy except that her blonde hair reached her waist. Her eyes were outlined in dark black eyeliner and she wore silver hoop earrings the size of teacup saucers.

"Mrs. Moore?" she had asked when Clara's mother opened the door, and without waiting for an answer, proceeded. "My name is Jenna McBride; this is my daughter Becca." She nodded to Becca, who stood next to her, staring down at her pigeon-toed feet, a silvery string of saliva hanging precariously from her chin. "I understand you have a daughter that is about Becca's age, and I thought it would be nice for the girls to meet each other. Become friends."

"She's a hippie, for heaven's sake!" Clara's mother said to her father over dinner that night.

He just laughed and said, "Well, there goes the neighborhood!"

Being Becca's best friend wasn't easy. Becca walked and

ran with awkward, jerking motions, drooled when she talked, and made loud, slurping noises when she ate. She hated to read books and didn't get jokes. Worst of all, if Becca got mad or didn't get her way, she'd punch anything in sight. Clara had the bruises to prove it.

The boys in the neighborhood, especially Becca's own brother, Jimmy, had plenty to make fun of when it came to Becca. Jimmy not only looked like a leprechaun with his curling red hair, and wildly freckled face, but he had the temperament of one as well. Clara didn't understand Jimmy at all. As Becca's big brother, he was supposed to protect her. Instead, he couldn't seem to resist teasing her. He was like a bee darting in on his prey, stinging quickly, darting away and then in again–relentless until he got bored.

The truth was, sometimes Becca drove Clara crazy, too. It hadn't seemed so bad at first, before they started school. But now, Becca felt like a weight tied to Clara's ankle. Clara had to watch out for Becca in school, to make sure no one teased her or was mean. She had to play games that she thought were too babyish now because Becca couldn't ride bikes or understand the rules of Monopoly. Occasionally, one of the younger girls in the neighborhood played with her and Becca after school. Clara envied the ease at which the younger girls got along with Becca. She wished maybe they would become best friends, and she could just quietly fade out of Becca's life.

When Clara reached the Millers' front lawn, she hopped gingerly across the hot pavement and onto the McBrides' front lawn, where she leapfrogged the yellow fire hydrant at the corner of the yard, before heading up the driveway toward the side door that led to the kitchen.

"Ha ha!!!" Jimmy's staccato laugh drifted out of the house. Clara stopped in the driveway and looked toward the house. There was the familiar drone of Becca's voice, but it was sharper, louder; she sounded mad. Becca and Jimmy were fighting again. Clara sat down on the lawn and picked at a dandelion. The voices rose and fell.

Clara wondered where Barbara, Mrs. McBride's niece, was. Mrs. McBride had hired Barbara to watch Jimmy and Becca after the last big fight. Clara had been in the house alone with Jimmy and Becca when the last big fight had erupted earlier in the summer. Jimmy had goaded Becca to the point where she was swinging wildly at him. Afraid that Becca would hurt herself or Jimmy, and unable to stop the fight, Clara had run across the street to the Millers', where she begged Mrs. Miller to call Mrs. McBride at work. When she ran back to the McBride house, Jimmy was on the phone with his mother, while Becca lay sobbing in a heap on the kitchen floor.

When Jimmy saw Clara, he snapped, "Get the hell out of here, tattletale!"

Clara ran all the way home, slamming the front door behind her. When her mother got home from work that afternoon, she'd already spoken to Mrs. McBride on the phone.

"Clara," her mother said with an exasperated sigh, "I don't like getting a call like that while I'm at work, and I'm sure Mrs. McBride didn't appreciate getting a call from Mrs. Miller over a little fight. People don't like tattletales, Clara."

Clara felt a stinging sensation, like a thousand bees, stabbing at her heart.

"Honestly, Clara, you need to think before you act. Now go up there and apologize to Mrs. McBride right now," her mother said sternly.

"But..." Clara wanted to explain that it hadn't been just a little fight.

"No buts," her mother interrupted. "March yourself up there right now and say you're sorry."

~

Jimmy's laugh wafted out of kitchen once more and Clara wondered if maybe she should give up on Becca and the sprinkler idea and just go home. She didn't want to be in the middle of another fight. It made her stomach ache. She thought about the Rule Book. She was convinced that everyone had a Rule Book about life, something that told you how to act in every situation. But she was missing her Rule Book, had lost it somewhere along the way. Somehow things made more sense when her father was alive. She didn't need a Rule Book when he was around. She pulled up a clump of grass absently. She didn't hear any yelling, just Jimmy's laugh. Maybe it would be okay. She stood up and edged slowly up the side steps to the kitchen door. She couldn't see inside the house; it was dark and the sun was blazing down onto the little porch. She moved closer to the screen door, cupped her hands around her eyes to block out the sun, and peered inside. Becca was standing in the kitchen, holding a steak knife in her hand.

"Yeah, you really scare me," Jimmy said to Becca as he turned away, laughing. Becca's right hand swung behind her, winding up for the blow, and then, with the force of her entire body, she stabbed Jimmy in the back.

Clara flinched. Jimmy's head pitched backward, but he stood very still, like a statue. A strange gurgling sound escaped his lips, and he dropped to his knees. He clutched at the air, as though he were grasping for something that wasn't there, and then fell face down, hitting his head on the small table where Becca's parents placed their mail and keys. The dark wooden handle of the knife stuck straight out from between his shoulder blades.

Becca stared at Jimmy. "Geddup!" she ordered. But Jimmy didn't move. "Stop it, Jimmy! Geddup right now," she screamed, but he still didn't move.

Clara's hands fell to her sides and she backed away from the screen door. She walked slowly down the stairs, down the driveway, onto the street. She didn't notice the heat from the pavement as it burned her feet. She turned into her own driveway and up the brick walkway to the front door. She opened it, and the cool darkness of the house greeted her.

She changed out of her bathing suit and into shorts and a T-shirt. She walked out the back door and down the long flight of stairs. Crossing the yard, she scrunched herself into one of the two swings on the rust-red swing set. Her bare feet brushed back and forth on the gray cement. In the corner of the cement pad was a list of names. Mike, Martha, Steve, Lenore, and Clara. All the people who'd been here the day her father had laid the cement for her swing set. Her father had handed her the stick and taught her how to spell her name that day, saying each letter aloud and gently reminding her how to form the letters with his finger in the air.

C-L-A-R-A. Clara.

After he'd installed the swing set, Clara had spent her entire summer playing in the back yard, swinging as high as she could, certain if she swung high enough, she'd be able to take off and fly.

Her favorite times were when her father grilled on the patio while she played. She imagined they were the only two people in the world. She'd watch him carefully light the charcoal briquettes and stand by the fire, turning the chicken breasts and thighs periodically as they browned and crisped, his face turning pink from the heat.

"Watch me, Daddy!" she'd call out as she turned cartwheel after cartwheel across the vast expanse of green lawn, finally stopping, wobbling and weaving with dizziness.

"That's terrific, Pumpkin!" he'd call back, smiling as he pushed the blond curl off his broad forehead.

She wished he were here today. He'd know what to do about Jimmy and Becca's fight. Fear stabbed at Clara's heart and stomach, sending rays of panic through her body. She shivered uncontrollably. She couldn't get the look of surprise on Jimmy's face as the knife hit, or Becca's wails, out of her head. She wished she could start the day all over. She thought she should pray, but couldn't think of what to pray for. "Dear God," she finally whispered, "somehow please make this all okay. I promise I'll be better from now on if you just please, please, please make this okay." She'd prayed the same thing, or something like it, after they'd rushed her father out of the house on a gurney, an oxygen mask on his blue face. God hadn't listened to her then. Sometimes she would tell herself that her father hadn't really died at all. She imagined he had just gone away on a really long trip or had amnesia like Sara Crewe's father, and one day he'd come back and everything would be back to normal again.

Clara heard the water turn on in the kitchen and looked up to see her mother's outline in the kitchen window. She was home from work, probably making tea. Clara used to know her mother was in the house because she sang as she went about her day. But Clara had not heard her mother sing since her father had died. Not a note. Now her mother just seemed sad and angry.

Clara stepped off the swing and made her way to the back stairs. As she climbed, voices drifted out of the kitchen. Her mother was talking to someone: Betty, her best friend. Clara heard her mother gasp and then say, "Oh, my God." Clara stopped midway up the stairs, her heart pounding. Her mother never said that, no matter how angry or upset she got. The worst Clara had ever heard her say was "Aw, heck!" or "Dagnabbit!" But never "Oh, my God."

"...they're probably going to have to institutionalize her," Betty was saying. "She doesn't even really know what she did. When Jenna got home, she was still trying to get him to wake up."

"Jenna turned a blind eye to what was happening with both of her children."

"Well, she's young, Martha," Betty sighed.

"She lets those two run wild while she's off working," Clara's mother said sharply. "And she doesn't even have to work. I'd love to stay home, but I don't have that luxury, and she's off working because she's bored at home."

"Clara didn't say anything to you?" Betty changed the subject. Clara's mother's disapproval of Jenna McBride's job was an old complaint.

"She was home when I got home, but I haven't spoken to her. I'm not sure she even knows what happened."

Clara stood frozen on the stairs. Should she go in? She crept slowly up the rest of stairs to the back door. She wondered if she could sneak in; avoid her mother and Betty altogether. She tried to open the screen door quietly, but it squeaked, and they both looked over at her.

"Hi," she said looking at her mother.

"Clara," her mother said, "I have some really sad news." The last time her mother had said this, it was to tell her that her father had died at the hospital. Clara had cried so hard her heart hurt, and she wondered if she'd die of a heart attack, too.

Clara waited.

"It's about Jimmy McBride," her mother finally said, looking hard at Clara. "There's been a very bad accident, and Jimmy's dead."

Dead. The word catapulted around Clara's brain. Dead.

She looked from her mother to Betty for confirmation. Betty nodded.

"He's dead?" Clara whispered. "H-How?"

"It was an accident," her mother said. "A terrible accident." She was silent for a moment. "Were you with Becca today?" she finally asked.

A strange, tingling sensation started in Clara's chest and moved quickly to her arms and legs. She looked at her mother and Betty, and it was as though she were underwater, seeing them through the wavy ripples of the ocean. "Why?" was all she could think of, all she could say. Why was everyone she knew dying?

~~~

The day of the funeral, Clara wore one of her school dresses–ivory, tan, and turquoise plaid on top, with a deep brown Peter Pan collar and skirt. It was a warm dress for August, but her mother told her it was the right dress for a funeral.

Outside of the church, her mother stopped her and pulled a small, plastic envelope out of her purse and removed a white, lace kerchief. She pinned it to Clara's hair before they entered the church. Clara was glad she didn't have to wear her Easter hat, with the elastic band that made her neck itch.

The church was cool and dark and crowded with Becca's family, as well as the families from the neighborhood and some of Jimmy's school friends. Becca's family sat in the first few pews. Mrs. McBride's black hat and veil made her look like pictures of Jackie Kennedy at the president's funeral. Mrs. McBride would probably like the thought that she looked like Jackie Kennedy. The only time Clara had really had any fun with Becca was when Mrs. McBride talked to them about movie stars. Mrs. McBride would talk to the girls for hours about her favorite movie stars and how she was going to meet them all one day. Her favorite was Tom Jones. She was supposed to see him in person this summer, and Mrs. McBride swore he was going to pick her out of the crowd, swoop into the audience and kiss her right on the lips.

Mr. McBride, his balding head bent, sat next to Mrs. McBride, with his arm wrapped around her shoulders. She rested her head on his shoulder, and sometimes she cried so hard it made Mr. McBride cry. Clara had never seen a man cry before.

Becca was not sitting with her parents. She was in the pew behind them, with her grandmother. She wore a black lace kerchief, which she kept reaching up and flinging behind her shoulders as though it were her hair. She looked like one of those bobble-head toy dogs, with her head in constant motion, as she greeted everyone in the church, smiling and waving as new people walked in. Her grandmother kept turning her around, leaning down and whispering in Becca's ear. And though Becca looked earnestly at her grandmother and nodded, she would soon be swiveling and bobbing again. It was the first time since Clara had known Becca that she was jealous of her. She wished she could forget Jimmy's death so easily.

After the funeral, as they drove home, Clara's mother turned to her. "Such a shame," she said. "I'm glad you weren't playing with Becca that day. I'm glad you didn't see what happened."

"Maybe I could have done something?" Clara asked quietly. "Gone for help. Like last time."

"Well, maybe. But it's just best that you aren't involved in this mess. It's not good to get into other people's business."

~~~

There was a tightness in her chest that made it hard for Clara to sleep that night. Slivers of streetlight escaped into her room where the shades didn't meet the windows, casting eerie shadows around her room.

Clara pushed the covers away and got up out of bed. She walked soundlessly out of her bedroom and across the hall to her mother's bedroom. She stood by the side of her mother's bed. She was relieved to hear her steady breathing; her mother had not died in her sleep. Clara looked at the picture of her father on the nightstand next to the bed, his khaki army cap covering his blonde curls. She used to think he looked happy in this picture, but tonight she thought he looked like he might be disappointed in her.

"Mom," she whispered, but her mother didn't stir. Clara dropped to her knees and rested her head against her mother's mattress.

"I'm scared. I'm scared you're gonna die and leave me. That God is gonna punish me. Because I saw it all, Mom. I saw Becca stab Jimmy. But I didn't know. I didn't know he'd die. I was just trying to do what you told me, minding my own business, not being a tattletale."

But she did know. She was right to get help during the first fight. She should have gotten help this time. The house creaked as it shifted and settled. Even if her mother woke up, Clara knew she wouldn't be able to help, wouldn't be able to make her feel better about what had happened.

She looked at her father's picture again. He didn't look disappointed, she decided, just sad.

Love & Lust

Wendy Lewis

No Words

Don't ask me to explain.
Because it is not in words
that I know what I want.

The smoothness of warm skin,
strong hands, thick fingers, ropy veins,
salt and sweat and breath.

Don't talk about what it means.
Just call me sweetheart,
and cut fresh vegetables
in piles of green and yellow
for my dinner.

Hold me tight enough
so that our heartbeats synchronize.
You can see it in the brown
of my eyes.

It's the vastness of the sky.
The changing seasons.
An opening of the heart.

Traci Post

Angels in the Garden

A timeless hush drifts over the garden at dusk; the untethered light of day slips into night. The stage is set. They are all in place, ready for the performance to begin. A moment in the twilight lingers on a whisper of air until finally the Angels begin their dance.

Swaying in the night breeze, long wispy strands of Mexican feather grass skip and dance to a rhythm only they can feel. Enlivened by the freedom of darkness, their moves are graceful and innocent. The dance is all their own.

Enormous golden boulders tinted with rings of cinnabar and limestone lay claim to their turf. These mighty Angels stand proud at the gates of the garden, bowing at the waist of the olives, kneeling at the feet of the blue oat grass. Their sheer weight holds the garden in place, their job done with the confidence and ease of those who know themselves. They understand their role in the universe. Secure and unwavering, they are majestic as all eternity is within them.

A white-winged creature flutters to the blushing pink blossom of Penstemon, pulsing life into the bud before giving in to the whim of fancy by which it lives, and floats away on the exhalation of the evening air. She waits for no one, her mind her own.

They've slipped under the garden gate, a whisper away from a touch of lips. The Angels pause, turn to watch. They revel in the glow emanating toward them from the quiet lovers. A caress of cheek sends golden sparks over the waiting Angels. A promise, unsaid, hangs in the air, until finally it is caught in the tide of life's immense sea. She waits, her heart no longer her own. He sees, hopes for so very much.

The enduring oak holds court on her corner of the stage. Everything revolves around her, toward her in the dusky shadows. In a moment of stillness her beauty rises up from the Earth. Everything is exactly as it should be.

Frosty green leaves clamor at the feet of long purple spires, their calming scent sweetening the breath of night. So subtle are these lavender cherubs, they are often overlooked with only their lingering fragrance to hint at their existence.

Tiny angels of Little John promise they will delight, too. But their thick, stubby stalks prevent their joining in the dance. Instead, they sulk, silent. Infants with so much hidden depth, waiting eternally for their time to come. But first fall, then winter must set before they are free to grow in the warm days of spring and long summer nights.

Dry, lifeless forms dot the landscape stage here and there. The dance quickens with death and rebirth. Their life is done in this angel capacity. Quickly forgotten, they are replaced, just as they wished. It was not their desire to leave a legacy of blackness over the garden. Instead, the gouges in the soil where they once thrived are quickly filled with new hopes for fresh life; the dazzling life of an Angel in the garden.

Two hearts merge under the thoughtful eyes of the Angels. Her voice soft and yielding she encourages him to harvest the love she nurtures for him and him alone. He leans closer, the warm flesh of his lips lingering on hers. He is already there, within her.

Long, long limbs of Salvia maraschino spread haphazardly at their own petulance. Confident in their beauty, nonchalant in their exquisite nature. Deep cherry-red blossoms light the night for all the Angels' eyes to see. They do not rely on the sun's luminescence, for their vision sees beyond the darkness to the eternal glow from within.

Standing guard at the perimeter of the garden Tagetes lemmonii strike into the night with bursts of yellow. They are the merriest of all Angels. Not whimsical like the grasses, nor stately like the trees, but effervescent with citrus-scented smiles and soft giggles. Their charm their greatest defense.

A smoky, green-hued river of grasses serenely flows along the soft mounds of fleshy earth. Her currents slow and methodic, time waits for her to catch up. Cascading soundlessly she is one with the earth. They are her Angels, for her alone. Bubbling around the boulders, a stream not yet ripe with the raging waters of snow melt in spring, she silently promises so much more.

Olive tree knows she has been granted more time in the garden. She knows there are no guarantees. Angels move through this world so rarely seen and acknowledged. While her trunk is scarred and raw from nature's wrath of heat and drought, she relishes the sight of nature's offspring growing with wild abandon. They are fearless, reckless in their youth. She keeps a watchful eye on their interaction with the surroundings. The wise olive is the one remaining touchstone from times gone by. As she heals, she bears fruit to nourish and sustain the serenading birds and frantic squirrels. She nurtures all those around her, as it is simply who she is.

The lilies gather in the orchestra pit. They fill the garden with songs of promise. Long flowing leaves reach down toward the dark earth, pulling their finest tunes from deep beneath the soil. Bursts of flowers sing and flirt with all who wander amidst the beauty. A chorus of melodious sighs lifts even the saddest of souls.

There are powers greater than all of us, Angels and humans. We see only the light, we hide from the darkness. And it is the hiding that enslaves us to the unknown. Just as the sun and moon can be in the same sky, and the garden has both life and death, our lives possess the light and dark. It does not have to be one or the other. Life is all around.

She looks into his eyes and feels the soft breath of his soul linger around her heart. She is home, there, reflected in his eyes. Tonight, their dance begins. Falling deep into their love, they feel the peace of eternal existence, in the Garden of Angels.

Two Step and Other Dances

Grace knew that George had hired her simply because she would fit into the uniform. It was hard enough to find a girl who wanted to waitress in this hot, dusty, little town, but to find one who also fit into the previous waitress's uniform was a bonus.

The pink uniform, with its dull white cuffs and apron, looked about as depressed as Grace felt. She hadn't come to Ranger to waitress. She had been headed to San Francisco. But when she stopped off in Ranger to fill her gas tank, her first thought was, this looked like a good place to get lost, and so it seemed like a good place to stay.

"Order up!" George yelled from behind the grill as he slid a plate of scrambled eggs, steak, and biscuits across the stainless steel shelf that separated the kitchen from the rest of the restaurant. He pulled the order ticket off the check spindle and slapped it down next to the plate. Grace retrieved the plate and grabbed a pot of hot coffee on her way to deliver the meal.

"More coffee?" she asked as she dropped the hot plate in front of the stranger.

"No, thanks." His soft voice did not have the twang she'd grown accustomed to these last three months. She hadn't seen him in the café before. He didn't have the hard, leathered look of most of the men from Ranger. His complexion was fair and his hair, the color of straw, was long and tapped his broad shoulders in shaggy waves.

"Ketchup or Tabasco?" she asked.

"No, thanks."

She placed the bill on the counter next to his plate.

"Thank you," she said and walked away.

The café was empty except for George and the stranger. It was ten o'clock–the day was half over for most of the men that lived and worked in Ranger. It was unusual to have anyone in the café at this time of the morning. Collecting the salt and pepper shakers from the tables to refill them, she glanced over at the stranger. There weren't too many strangers in Ranger, which was why her arrival in the little town had created such a stir. The only people that typically came to Ranger were visiting relatives who usually escaped the boredom of the town as quickly as they could fulfill their family obligation. Maybe he had run away, too.

"Grace!" George yelled from the kitchen. "What the hell are you doing?"

Grace looked down and realized she had poured salt into all of the shakers–even the pepper shakers. The stranger was looking at her too; a slight smile crossed his face. She smiled back, shrugged her shoulders and began emptying out the half salt-half pepper shakers in the sink. He turned back to his eggs without a word.

When she was finished, Grace turned off the tap.

"More coffee?" she asked.

"No, thank you."

"Where are you heading to?" she asked.

He looked up from his eggs.

"L.A.," he finally answered.

"Is that where you're from?"

"It's where I live now," he said, "but I spend a lot of time traveling around. I'm a musician."

"Huh, a musician," she mused. "Would I know of anything you've done?"

"Probably not. I mostly play back-up guitar, vocals, that kind of thing for guys more rich and famous than I'll ever be."

"What kind of music?"

"Country."

"Mmmm." She pursed her lips and wrinkled her nose, her head tilted slightly. "Not a big fan of country music," she said.

"Sorry."

"That's okay," he laughed. "It's got a special appeal."

"What's Los Angeles like?" she asked

He took a sip of coffee. "Fast...busy...crowded...tough place to get a break."

"I bet it's a good place to get lost," she said.

"You lookin' to get lost?"

"Maybe."

"Little quiet here for you?"

"Yes, a bit too quiet sometimes."

"How long have you been here?"

"I'm pretty new in town, just about three months."

"Where you from?" he asked.

"Providence...originally." It was the truth, she thought, even if she hadn't lived there for the past seven years.

He nodded, then held out his hand. "I'm Ted, Ted Wheeler."

She took his hand and a little pulse of electricity passed through her.

"Pleased to meet you, Ted; I'm Grace."

"Just Grace?" he asked.

"Just Grace."

~~~

At two o'clock her shift was finally over. She grabbed her car keys from the drawer under the cash register where she kept them with her wallet and sunglasses and headed for the door.

"Bye-bye, George!" she called.

The little bell tinkled when she opened the front door into the heavy, hot, afternoon air. She untied her apron while she walked toward her car. She stopped in the middle of the parking lot, looked around and then at her car again. It was definitely her car, a green Honda Civic, but the stranger from this morning, Ted, was leaning up against it. She put her hand to her forehead to shade her eyes.

"Hi!" he called out to her. He was wearing a black cowboy hat and Ray-Bans that he took off when he saw her.

"Hi," she answered doubtfully. "What do you want?"

He smiled. "I just wanted to talk to you a bit...get to know you...you know?"

"You could have talked to me in the café."

"You were working, and besides, I had an appointment in town."

She brushed a few loose hairs behind her ear. The dark strands refused to stay in her ponytail. "How'd you know that was my car?" she asked as she walked toward him.

"I asked your boss."

"George?"

He nodded, his tall, muscular body leaning easily against her car. She looked away. The heat from the parking lot rose up in tiny waves. A train whistled in the distance. "So what do you want to talk about?" she asked, looking back at him.

"I was hoping you might consider having dinner with me tonight," he said.

"Dinner?" She was surprised by the invitation. She hadn't received an invitation from anyone for anything since she'd arrived in Ranger. Not that she had put herself out socially. She'd spent most of the last three months trying to disappear into the ordinariness of the town. It might be nice to have some company for dinner for a change, and he didn't look dangerous. What did she have to lose?

"Okay," she said finally. "When and where?"

"How about Cattleman's at seven o'clock?"

"Cattleman's at seven. Okay, I'll meet you there," she said, pulling the car keys out of her uniform pocket.

He stepped aside. "See you then," he said, closing the door for her.

~~~

The sun poured into the little canary-colored house and danced off the stark white walls, making the house surprisingly bright and unbearably hot during the day. Grace opened the windows to let the slight breeze in. Although she had lived in the house for almost three months now, having rented it shortly after she'd arrived in Ranger, there were few signs of Grace in the house.

A stack of books, a half-painted canvas propped up on a make-shift easel, a palette with dried paints–dark greens, grays, black, ochre, and crimson. Grace had left a stack of paintings in the garage in North Carolina. Paintings that got progressively darker, filled with images of people being swallowed whole into dark abysses. Images that frightened her. Grace's art had always been her refuge, her way to think things through, but now, here in Ranger, she couldn't paint. She would stare at the blank canvas for hours and then put her brush down and walk away.

The tiny house was furnished with the landlord's family's attic and basement finds: a sagging couch covered with a sage green slipcover; an old leather chair, smelling slightly of cigarette smoke and bearing the indentations of a seat and back that had probably sat in it every night for years; a mismatched assortment of tables and lamps reflecting an interest in Colonial America. She flopped down on the couch. She wanted to sleep–just drift away into the warm fog of the afternoon. But her mind wouldn't switch off long enough to let sleep in.

She shouldn't have agreed to meet Ted for dinner tonight. Maybe she just shouldn't show up. She quickly dismissed the idea; she wanted to see him again. She closed her eyes and tried to remember his voice, his smile, so different from Hal's nasal twang and perpetual worried look.

She stood up from the couch and walked into the tiny bedroom in the back of the house, peeled off her sad uniform and headed to the bathroom for a cool shower.

~~~

She pulled her car into the parking lot of Cattleman's shortly before seven. It was crowded but the crowd would thin soon enough–almost no one here began dinner at seven o'clock. She walked through the double doors and looked around. She didn't see Ted anywhere. Had she been stood up? She looked at her watch–it was 7:03. Maybe she shouldn't have been so punctual–did that make her look too eager?

"Hello, Grace," she heard his soft voice behind her.

She turned and then looked away nervously. "Hi, Ted."

"I've got us a table already, if you'd like to sit down," he said, his hand pressed lightly against the small of her back, leading her to the main dining room before she could answer.

She slid into a booth in the corner of the restaurant and looked around at the red carpet, the diamond pattern of the seats, the silk plants in the boxes that separated the waiters' station from the diners.

"Not much on ambience," he said, following her gaze.

"That's okay," she said. "It's the only game in town. I've actually never eaten here before, anyway, so it's new for me."

"Never eaten at a Cattleman's before? Tsk, tsk," he said in mock horror. "Next you'll be telling me you've never two-stepped either!"

"Two-stepped? What's that?"

"You're pulling my leg. You've never two-stepped?" he asked.

Puzzled, she looked at him.

"Danced!" he exclaimed.

"Oh, no, I don't dance," she said. "My family always teases me about how badly I dance. You know, Grace-less on the dance floor...that sort of thing."

"Anyone can two-step," he said. "In fact, there's got to be a place in a cowtown like this where we can take a turn on the dance floor."

"There's the Tumbleweed," she offered hesitantly.

"Great, we'll go over there after dinner tonight and work off some of this meal. I'll show you."

"I don't know. I've got to be at work at six sharp tomorrow morning. George is very unhappy when I'm late."

"One dance," he promised. "Then I'll let you go home."

He was irresistible.

"Okay," she agreed.

~~~

The Tumbleweed was just on the outskirts of Ranger in what used to be a feed storage shed. Now it housed a bar, a band, and a mechanical bull. In Ranger, this was where you came to have a beer, listen to some music, take a turn with your partner around the dance floor, and maybe ride the mechanical bull if you'd had a bit too much to drink, although that was usually left to the young men who were out to impress a girl.

The air was warm and smoky, and voices competed with the Country and Western band for attention. Grace looked around at what seemed like hundreds of people pressed into the bar and on the dance floor. She hadn't realized there were so many people in Ranger. Their faces flushed and sweaty with drink and dance, they leaned into one other, laughing, talking, and kissing.

Ted led Grace right to the dance floor. "Wait a minute, aren't you going to even offer me a drink?" she resisted, pulling on his hand.

"You said you had to get home; you've got an early day tomorrow," he called back to her, firmly holding onto her hand as he wove through the crowd on the dance floor.

"Well, I've got time for one drink!" she insisted.

"You'll be fine," he said as he turned toward her and took her in his arms. They moved awkwardly around the dance floor. He attempted to guide her, but if he moved left, she moved right; if he moved forward, she did, too. She stepped on his foot and laughed nervously, and then just stopped.

"Really, Ted, this is nice of you, but I can't do this. I've never been able to dance; I'm such a disaster when it comes to this stuff." Her cheeks burned with embarrassment.

"Close your eyes," he said.

"What?" she peered up at him.

"Close your eyes," he commanded again. "Now just listen to the music for a minute. Listen to the beat, one-and-two, three-and-four, one-and-two, three-and-four. Now, feel the pressure I'm putting on your back? I'm telling you which way I'm going to move so that you can follow me. Okay?"

She opened her eyes and nodded.

"Let's try it again," he said.

He began to move, slowly at first, still counting "one-and-two, three-and four..." softly into her ear. Although she was far from ready for the Ballroom Semi-finals, she managed not to step on his feet this time. When the music ended, everyone stopped to applaud the band and Grace started to move away.

"Whoa, where you going?" Ted asked.

"You said one dance. That was your one dance."

"That was because you said you had an early morning and

that's all you had time for. That reasoning went out the window when you asked me to buy you a drink. You've got time for another dance."

"You're just trying to torture me, aren't you?" she said. The music started again.

"Yup. Now get back here and dance."

To Grace's great relief, the band took a break after their second dance, and they headed toward the bar to get a couple of beers and find a table.

"How long will you be in Ranger?" Grace asked.

"Just a few days," Ted said. "I just finished a tour and had some business to take care of before heading back to L.A."

"What business could you possibly have in Ranger?" she asked.

"Maybe you're my business," he said.

"Pretty boring business."

"You have any family, Grace? Brothers? Sisters?" he asked.

"Nope," she said. "Only child."

"That's too bad," he said, "you gotta have someone to complain to about your parents...someone who really gets it. Otherwise, people are always telling you how great your folks are, and you're wondering what kind of slug you are that they annoy you so much."

She laughed, "Oh, so you know my parents!"

"They're everybody's parents, I guarantee you."

"How about you?" she asked.

"A brother. He lives in Nashville. He's married with two kids...boys. Ted and Nate."

"Hmmm, a namesake. You must be close," she said.

"Yeah, we are." He looked out across the bar, "You planning on staying in Ranger?" he finally asked.

She worked on the label of the bottle, slowly peeling away the corners.

"Eventually I'd like to get to San Francisco, but for now this is working for me."

"What's in San Francisco?"

"I don't know."

"You know, Grace," he said, "my Grandmother used to say running from something gets you nothin' but tired. Running to something usually gets you a soft place to land."

"A little kitchen wisdom from Grandma, huh?" she laughed. "I'm just looking for something, and I haven't found it...yet, anyway," she said, looking down at her beer. "Wanna dance?"

"Now I know I'm treading on dangerous ground, if you're asking me to dance."

He let her lead him to the dance floor.

It was late when she arrived home that evening. She lay on her bed staring up at the cracks in the ceiling. It was too hot for midnight, and her T-shirt was sticking to her. She couldn't fall asleep again, and the heat had nothing to do with it. She rolled over onto her side. She thought about Ted's arms around her, the way it felt to dance with him. Damn Ted. She punched her pillow.

~~~

"Shit," Grace sighed as she dropped another plate. She took a quick sideways glance to see if George had noticed. He had. She ran into the back to get the dustpan and broom and was surprised when she came back to find Ted sitting at the counter.

"Hi there," he said.

"Hi," she said, sweeping up the remains of the shattered plate.

"7:30 - that's a bit early for a city slicker like you, isn't it?"

"I couldn't sleep. It was too hot, I guess." He hesitated. "I was hoping I'd see you."

She blushed, pushed a stray hair behind her ear, and smoothed down her uniform. "What'll it be?" she asked.

"Steak and eggs, scrambled, biscuits, and coffee."

Grace walked over to the coffee station and picked up a pot of coffee. She was overzealous in the pouring, and the black liquid sloshed over the rim of the cup onto the counter. "I'm sorry," she said, pulling the towel from her apron waistband and wiping the counter. "I'm tired. I didn't sleep very well last night, either," she confessed.

"I'm sorry."

"No, not your fault."

Ted watched as she wiped up the coffee. "Grace, are you busy this afternoon?" It was almost an absurd question; she was never busy in the afternoons. But he didn't know that.

"No, no plans."

"I thought you might like to go riding."

"Riding?" she asked. "Riding what?"

"You live in Texas, girl. What do you think people ride here?"

"A horse?" Her voice was filled with dread.

"Yes, a horse."

"I don't know how to ride a horse."

"That's okay," he said. "Trust me, this will be easier than dancing. We'll find you an old nag that can't even break into a gallop." He looked at her as though he could will her to say yes. "I'd like to get to know you better, Grace."

She sighed. "Okay. Don't ask me why, but I'll give it a try."

"Great!"

"Order up!" George yelled. Grace turned, and George caught her eye but looked away without saying anything.

~~~

Ted knocked on her door at three o'clock sharp. He was wearing his black cowboy hat and holding a smaller tan one with a dark leather band.

"Hi, there," she said, feeling very shy. She hadn't dated in a very long time. "Come in."

He stepped onto the threshold of the small house and glanced around at the sad furniture. The half-painted canvas caught his eye.

"You paint," he said, walking over to it.

"Yes, well, I used to...I dabble now, I guess. I mean, I can't seem to find the motivation to paint these days. I guess it's just too damn hot."

"Oh, that reminds me," he said as he handed her the hat, "I've got a little something for you."

She looked at the hat but didn't reach for it. "I really couldn't accept such a nice gift."

"Well, it's really more than a gift," he said. "You'll bake in the sun out there. You need something to protect you. Unless you already have one?"

She nodded and looked at the hat. It was just a hat, not a commitment. She reached out for it and put it on.

～

At the Lightfoot Stables, just west of town, Ted was true to his word and found her a gentle, quiet Chestnut mare named Rosie. The horses were saddled up by a young, russet-haired stable boy whose freckled skin was already tanned to a fine leather. Ted helped Grace mount Rosie and then swung with ease onto his own mount, a Paint named Napoleon.

They hadn't ridden far, maybe a half an hour out, when Ted stopped his horse and reached for Rosie's reins.

"Look at this place," he said as he dismounted and walked around to the side of her horse to help her down. "It's beautiful!"

He led the horses over to the shade of a mesquite tree and wound the bridles in some scrub brush beneath it. He took her hand, and they followed a stream that meandered gently through the countryside. They came to a gnarled old oak whose craggy branches embraced a flat rock nestled against it.

Grace lay down on the rock; its warmth penetrated her back and arms. Exhausted from the lack of sleep the night before, content to be with Ted, she closed her eyes and drifted into a half-asleep / half-awake state. She heard Ted's footsteps crunch the dry ground and then a splash of water. She propped herself up on her elbows. He was crouched by the stream, his hat in one hand, splashing water on his face and through his sandy hair with the other. She wanted to be the water, touching him. He stood, turned toward her, and smiled.

He sat down next to her on the rock. Impulsively, she reached out and touched his warm, wet face, his forehead with the little crease between his eyebrows, the laugh lines around his cornflower eyes. She brushed her thumb back and forth over his lips, the palm of her hand resting gently on his chin, which had the merest hint of a cleft. He reached up and drew her hand to his lips, gently kissing the calloused, red palms. He looked steadily into her eyes, searching...for what? What was he looking for? What did he want to find?

She placed both hands on his chest, and she could feel the steady thump of his heartbeat. He drew her to him, and she rested her head on his shoulder. He was strong, sturdy, like the tree.

"I wish I had a place like this," she said, but she didn't mean the rock, nestled under the tree by the stream.

She looked up at him, and a tickle of thrill rushed from her throat to her heart. He brushed the ever-loose tendril of hair away from her face and kissed her. At that moment, there was no Ranger, no Hal, no Providence, no running; there was just Ted. And where she ended and he began, she couldn't tell.

How long they sat there, how long they kissed, she couldn't be sure. When she opened her eyes, the sun was low on the horizon. Muted shades of gray, blue, and purple reflected off the water, turning it to a shimmer. Rosie and Napoleon nickered, and an almost imperceptible shiver ran down Grace's spine.

"Are you cold?" he asked.

It wasn't cold that had caused her to shiver, it was the thrill of being so near him, but she said nothing, for fear he would let her go.

Hugging her closer, he brushed his hands up and down her back and arms. "We'd better go." He stood up and reached out his hand.

~~~

As they rode back into town, Grace didn't want to stop thinking about Ted, about what had just happened and what it meant. But she couldn't prevent Hal from creeping into her mind. She felt guilty. The day she left, she'd just packed up her clothes and a few books and was gone. No note, no phone call, no regrets. She just couldn't stand it any longer, couldn't stand her life with him. He was so needy, so dependent on her that he was drowning her.

After she'd had her appendix removed, Hal had sat by her hospital bed in the cold, plastic chair. Hour after hour he watched her with the familiar look of worry on his face, his hands fidgeting.

"Hal, go home," she finally said. "I need the rest and so do you."

She wondered why such an innocent statement caused him to look like a puppy that had just been kicked. He was always finding an unintended hurt in things she said. He leaned over, kissed her on the forehead and quietly left the room. If he had been a dog, his tail would've been between his legs.

Her roommate at the hospital watched Hal as he left the room. "He loves you very much," she said, a slight tinge of envy in her voice. It was a common reaction to Hal. Most of her friends thought she was the luckiest woman around to have such an attentive husband.

"Yes," Grace said, turning away. "I'm very lucky."

This one incident was a microcosm of their entire life together. He wasn't overly attentive because she was sick and he was scared. He always acted that way, too anxious to please her, even if it meant sacrificing his own happiness.

She'd once told him, "You don't always have to agree with me, Hal. It's okay to disagree. In fact, it's healthy to disagree."

But Hal would not disagree with her. She was the third Mrs. Harold Anderson, and he wasn't going to blow it this time.

She hadn't actually loved Hal when she married him. She was twenty-one and anxious to get out of her parents' house, out from under their bone-crushing control. When he asked her to marry him, she'd said "yes" immediately. Her apprehension had grown as their wedding day neared, but she dismissed her misgivings as normal pre-wedding jitters. She focused instead on the fact that she'd be getting off of Rose Street and out of Providence altogether, since they'd be moving to Hal's hometown in North Carolina. She didn't care if he was from Timbuktu as long as he got her off of Rose Street.

She'd never told Hal she was unhappy, so she guessed he'd been surprised, shocked really, by her abandonment. She imagined the look on his face as he walked through the house, coming to the realization that she had left. He'd probably cried. He would have called her friends to ask what they knew. Since she hadn't told anyone, they'd be of little help.

She supposed he could find her if he really wanted. She hadn't tried to hide her trail—she'd taken her car, used her credit cards, signed into hotels and motels using her own name.

Now, she inexplicably found herself in Ranger, Texas, of all places. No Hal, but no life either. And how could she ever explain all of this to Ted? What a mess.

~~~

It was Wednesday, Grace's day off. She sat at the wobbly pine kitchen table reading the paper, with a sweating glass of ice tea. It was five o'clock, and she had managed to while the day away without accomplishing much. She had hoped Ted would call and was so distracted by the thought that she couldn't concentrate on much of anything else.

As the day wore on and the phone didn't ring, doubts began to creep in. Had she moved too fast yesterday? She shouldn't have initiated the kiss. That was a mistake. Maybe after spending more time with her, Ted hadn't found her all that interesting after all. It had been years since she'd been on a date. Maybe you were supposed to act differently. But then, how old was Ted? Forty-two? Forty-three? How would he know how to act on a date? Maybe he dated a lot. He hadn't really said.

Maybe he was married. Oh, God. What if he's married? Maybe he's separated, too. Could he be gay? No, definitely not gay. A gay man would never kiss her like *that*. And he did kiss her like *that*. Oh, God, he must have been attracted to her...you don't kiss somebody like *that* if you're not attracted to them.

So why hasn't he called? Maybe he had some business to

take care of. He said he had business here. That must be it. He's tied up on business. She needed to wait until after five o'clock. That's when most things close down. He'll call this evening. Just wait.

As the clock ticked the minutes past five, doubt once again crept in. The knock at the door at 6:45 startled her. She couldn't help feel a surge of hope that it was Ted, although she told herself it was probably the paperboy. To her delight, Ted was standing on the front porch, grocery bag in one hand and guitar in the other.

"Hi. I brought dinner," he said, raising the grocery bag slightly. "I was betting you'd be home."

"Hi, c'mon in," Grace said, swinging the screen door open, acutely aware of her ratty Cirque du Soleil t-shirt and gray sweats, her dark hair twisted up on top of her head, held in place with a huge black plastic clip, and no make-up. Although she had showered in the morning, she felt like a damp, musty rag. "Wow, I wasn't really expecting you."

"That was the point; it was supposed to be a surprise."

"I'm definitely surprised. Make yourself at home; I need a minute to pull myself together."

"You look pretty pulled together to me," Ted said as he dropped the guitar in the living room and walked toward the little kitchen with its green and white tiled floor.

"Wine?" he asked, pulling a bottle of red out of the grocery bag.

"That'd be great," she called from the bedroom. She frantically pulled off her t-shirt and sweatpants. She grabbed a pair of jeans and her favorite apple green blouse from the closet. She ran into the bathroom and splashed herself with warm water, spritzed on some China Rain, and quickly applied some eye shadow, mascara and blush. She wished she'd shaved her legs that morning. She ran the brush through her hair and slipped on a pair of sandals.

He had found the wine glasses and poured her a glass of wine. Handing her the glass, he directed her to one of the ladder-back chairs at the kitchen table. She sat cross-legged on the chair, marveling at the sight of him in her small kitchen. He pulled pots and pans out of the pine cupboards. The kitchen had been furnished with a hodge-podge of mismatched plates, pans, and utensils, enough to cook a decent meal if not to create a beautiful presentation. He had laid an assortment of brightly colored vegetables and a butcher-paper wrapped package of meat on the white Formica countertop.

"And now, Ted's world famous steak and salad dinner," he announced.

"You're going to cook?" she asked.

"Of course I'm going to cook."

"I've never known a man who cooked before," she said.

"You know George," he said.

"That's different. He does it for a living," she explained. "I guess what I mean is I've never had a man cook for me before."

"That's too bad. It can be a very seductive experience."

She had no doubt of that.

She looked out the large, paned window of the kitchen onto the little back yard. "When do you have to head back to L.A.?"

"Soon," he said. "I have a few more days here and then I'll need to get back."

"You know," she said turning back to him, "I really don't know all that much about you. I mean, I know that you're a musician, that you live in L.A. and travel around a lot. You have a brother and two nephews in North Carolina. You have some business in Ranger right now but beyond that..."

"I could say the same about you," he said. "Let's see, I know that you've been in Ranger about three months now, you're an artist, and a waitress, an only child, you hate to dance, but you're a pretty fabulous kisser." He walked over, and tipping her face up with his hand, he leaned down and kissed her. She flushed. Oh, God, if she told him the truth, he'd run so fast. It was enough to scare any sensible man away.

"Okay," he said turning back to chopping his onion, "what can I tell you about myself? Let's see.... well, I was married once."

"You were?" she perked up.

"Yes, but we divorced about 10 years ago now. I don't think too much about her."

"What happened? I mean, do you mind me asking?"

"No," he said, "I don't mind. I came home one day and there she was, sitting in the living room, her packed suitcase on the floor next to her. Honestly, she looked so pretty, I thought my heart would just break. I knew right then she was leaving me. Worse yet, I knew it wouldn't take much to get her to stay." He stopped, seeming lost in thought. "But for the life of me, at the time, I couldn't figure out what that not much was."

"Sometimes, it's hard to know what someone else wants from you," she said. "Sometimes they just want too much."

"Yeah, well, I don't think it was that complicated with Nellie and me. I think I was just too absorbed in what I was doing to really pay attention to what she wanted. I hope I know better by now."

~~~

After dinner, Ted picked up his guitar, and they moved onto the little front porch. The night air had cooled down, and it was quiet in town. Ted sat on the top step, and Grace sat on the porch swing, her feet curled under her. She had never before heard the tune he played. It sounded Spanish and romantic and hung on the air for a moment before evaporating. In the distance, coyotes yelped and howled as though they were singing back-up. The music, the wine, and a full stomach, were taking over; she felt sleepy. She thought she might float away.

"Grace," Ted said.

"Yes."

"I have to tell you something," he said, "and you're not going to like it."

Her hand jerked involuntarily, spilling the contents of her wine glass, drenching her hand. She set the glass down with a hollow clink. She was suddenly on full alert.

"I'm not just a musician, Grace."

She waited, curiosity playing out in her mind. So he had lied to her about his profession. He was obviously something less interesting than a musician...what could be so terrible that he'd need to hide it from her? Her mind quickly ran down the list: a garbage man, a nuclear power plant operator, a used car salesman, or a lawyer?

He continued playing, watching his hands intently as they moved across the strings of the guitar. "I'm a private detective," he said finally.

She sat frozen on the swing.

"I came here to find you."

"Find me?" she whispered.

"Your husband, Hal, hired me to find you." He stopped playing and put the guitar down.

"He shouldn't have bothered. I'm not going back." She was surprised at how calm she sounded.

"I have to tell him where you are, Grace." The small crease between his eyebrows deepened.

"So all of this was just part of your job...to make sure it was me...the dancing and riding? The dinner and tonight?"

"No, no!" he stood up and walked over to her, kneeling next to the swing, he tried to take her into his arms but she pushed him away and ran to the front door.

"How could you?" she demanded.

He stood. "I meant to just walk away after I found you at the café. I knew it was you, but there was something about you...I wanted to find out why you left, I wanted to know...I just couldn't walk away once I saw you."

"So why didn't you just ask?" She tried to read his expression.

"You wouldn't have told me anything," he said.

"I thought about it, but I didn't know if I could trust you. I guess I was right." She grabbed at the door handle.

He put his hand over hers, stopping her from opening the door. "Grace, that's not fair. Grace, stop, please. We need to talk about this!"

"There's nothing to talk about. You got what you came here for. Tell Hal that you found me. Tell him where he can find me. Except he won't find me here, and you know that as well as I do."

Ted grabbed her shoulders. "I know. I know if I let go of you right now that you're going to run again, and I don't want to lose you."

"God forbid you lose your fee," she hissed.

"That's not what I mean, Grace," he said, their faces just inches apart. "Don't you get it? This isn't about the money. This isn't about the case. It's about you and me. What you're starting to mean to me. What I think I'm starting to mean to you."

"Don't kid yourself, Ted. I was just looking for a little company." She hoped it hurt; she meant it to. He didn't let go of her.

"I don't believe that, and I don't think you do either," he said quietly. "Listen to me, Grace, listen to me. There has to be a way to work this out for everyone. If I didn't care, why would I have told you who I was, what I was doing?"

"We're done, Ted. Actually, we never even started," she said, pulling away.

She yanked the screen door open and ran inside, slamming the front door behind her and locking it. She leaned against the door, quietly listening. If it were Hal, he would be knocking on the door, begging her to open it, to talk to him. Ted was not that kind of guy. She heard the solid sound of his footsteps as he walked across the porch, picked up his guitar and walked slowly down the stairs. She sank to her knees and wept. She couldn't remember the last time she had cried like this–an all-out sobbing, where everything grabs for the surface, the fears, frustrations, anger. She cried so hard that her chest ached. She had to will herself to stop. She was suddenly cold. She pulled an afghan off the sofa and wrapped it around herself.

"How could he?"

But another thought was pushing its way in–how could she? He had kept his purpose a secret from her, but before it had gone too far, he had confessed the truth to her. When was she planning to confess her truth to him? When was she planning to tell him that she'd left her husband without a word? The timing had never seemed right. When was she supposed to spill the beans–between dinner and dessert? "Hey, thanks so much, dinner has been great. By the way, I left my husband of seven years without a word. Pass the cream, please?"

No, but she could have found the time, made the time. She

was afraid he'd bolt, so it had been easier to say nothing, be mysterious. But she hadn't been a mystery; he had known the whole time.

She groaned, "How embarrassing!"

She thought back on all the times over the last few days that he had opened the door and she refused to cross the threshold. He wasn't the coward; she was. She hadn't been able to face Hal, and now she was running from Ted. He was right; she'd spent her whole life running, and now she was nothing but tired and alone.

She got up slowly and walked to the bathroom. Her eyes were red and puffy, her nose stuffy. She splashed her face with cold water.

It surprised her to realize that she had wanted a chance with Ted, a chance to be in love, really in love. To have a relationship with someone for no other reason than she loved being with him.

Well, she couldn't change things with Ted now. She had pretty successfully killed any chance she might have had with him. But she could fix things with Hal and get on with her life.

She walked into the living room, picked up the phone and dialed.

"Hello?" She almost didn't recognize Hal's voice; it sounded strange and distant, like someone unconnected to her.

"Hal? It's Grace."

"Grace? Where are you? I've been worried sick."

"I'm really sorry, Hal." She meant it. "I'm fine. I just needed some time," she hesitated, "and space." It sounded so clichéd, but it was the truth, and only the truth would do now, for herself as well as Hal.

~~~

She sat in the living room of the little yellow house, her bags packed, waiting for her cab. She'd sold the Honda to Cody at Ranger Auto Repair for $500. With 136,000 miles on it, it wouldn't make the trip to San Francisco. It had taken

her only a day to wrap up the last three months of her life. She hadn't seen or heard from Ted, not that she expected to.
She wondered if she'd miss Ranger. If she'd look back at this time in her life and say, "That's when I really grew up." She didn't feel very grown-up right now. Apprehensive was more like it. For the first time in her life, she was on her own and couldn't blame anyone else for her unhappiness but herself. But, by the same token, no one could claim her happiness except her.

Gravel crunched under tires and she heard the hum of an engine. She stood to gather her bags. There was a knock on the door before she could reach it. Most cab drivers she'd dealt with in the past thought honking their horn was the polite way to inform customers they'd arrived.

"Just a minute!" she yelled as she opened the door.

"Ted!" She couldn't believe he had come. "Please, please come in."

"Looks like you're heading out," he said as he walked into the living room.

"Yeah, well, trying to clean up the mess I've made of my life."

"Life is like a thump-ripe melon. So sweet and such a mess."

"More kitchen wisdom?" she asked.

He laughed. "No, a bit of Country-Western wisdom."

They were silent.

"Heading to San Francisco?" he asked.

"Yes," she answered. "Is your business finished?"

"I resigned the case this morning."

"I see." She was surprised and a little relieved.

"It seems you took care of some business, too," he said.

She looked confused.

"Hal didn't seem surprised to get my call."

"Oh," she said, with recognition. "Yes, we talked last night. He'll be okay." She stopped and then added, "So will I."

"I'll be heading for L.A. in the morning."

"It'll be nice to get home, I bet."

"You know, Grace, L.A. isn't so far from San Francisco."

"No," she said.

"A short plane flight. Less than an hour."

She didn't answer.

"I was just thinking that it wouldn't be that hard for us to see each other now and again. See if there's anything for us."

"You're not ready to give up and run?"

"Well, it's better to have it all out in the open," he said. "It's not good to have secrets between friends."

"Friends," she said. It was hard to hide her disappointment.

"Maybe more," he said. He walked over, took her in his arms, and held her for a long moment. "Can I take you to the airport?" he finally asked.

"I have a cab coming," she said.

"I ran into him outside. I gave him a twenty and sent him on his way," he grinned, obviously pleased with himself.

"Well, then, yes, I could use a ride," she said.

He picked up her suitcase and wrapped his arm around her shoulders, and they walked out of the house in Ranger together.

Sex and Chocolate

Chocolate is better than sex.

Aside from the obvious differences in taste and texture, chocolate has the dubious advantage of lasting forever on the hips.

Mandy sighed softly as she stared at the gift box of chocolates sitting on the edge of her coffee table. Tightly pressing her lips together, she raised her newspaper so she couldn't see the white box. Quickly leafing through the Life section, she found her horoscope, to read what her day should have been like.

If you want to attract that strong, gorgeous prospect, exhibit your own strength and compassion. Fight the temptation to procrastinate; once you begin, the battle is half over.

Lowering the paper just enough to catch sight of the box out of the corner of her eye, Mandy contemplated the meaningfully vague statements. The first couldn't be about a man. Mandy had just removed all evidence of Calvin ever being in her apartment or a part of her life.

∼

The evening had started innocently enough. Putting the final touches on her makeup for a date with Calvin, Mandy smiled at her reflection in the mirror. She thought about the first time Calvin had asked her on a date.

Calvin was her best friend and college housemate long before their relationship became even more intimate. Mandy and Calvin could tell each other anything. They often talked until the wee hours of the night when they were supposed to be studying. Since they loved to cook together, going out to dinner was usually an impromptu outing with their other housemates or friends. Mandy thought it was a little strange when Calvin half-suggested, half-asked her to dinner several days in advance. The night of the date, she was even more surprised when she found Calvin clean-shaven and wearing his best jeans with his only button-down shirt, waiting downstairs in their living room.

All through dinner at their favorite restaurant they talked about important friendships–theirs, other close friends', and past friendships and romances. It wasn't until they were walking home that Calvin worked up the courage to tell Mandy how he felt about her, following an awkward statement of how he had only said the same three magic words to one other woman. Mandy stopped walking, unsure of how to respond. Calvin stood in front of her, searching her face. After a few seconds of awkward silence, he grabbed her hand, leaned in and kissed her softly on her half open lips. To her amazement, Mandy found herself kissing Calvin back. At that moment she knew she loved him, too.

After being inseparable for nearly three years, it was now becoming difficult to see each other. A few months earlier they had moved to Toronto, where they had separate careers and separate apartments since Calvin decided they needed some space after living together for so long. Calvin moved into an apartment near where he grew up in Etobicoke while he encouraged Mandy to live uptown at Yonge and Eglinton. The neighborhood was nicknamed "Young and Eligible" for its abundance of restaurants, martini bars and nightclubs usually filled with the twenty-somethings living in the area. Since Mandy was new to Toronto, she enjoyed having that excitement right outside her door.

When Calvin arrived for their date that evening, he presented her with the small gift box and joked about how she didn't need him around when she had chocolates.

"I'm not that bad," she insisted. "Besides, I'd much rather have you."

Straightening her collar, he said, "Jen and Dave are meeting us at the restaurant. We better get going."

"Oh."

"I didn't think you'd mind."

"Well, I haven't seen you all week, I thought... I didn't think it was going to be a double date."

"Jen wanted to do something with us tonight so I invited them along. We're only going to dinner and a movie. No big deal."

All through dinner, the couples talked about mundane topics like work, movies, and their plans for upcoming summer weekends. By dessert, Jen, Dave and Calvin were reminiscing about their high school days and friends, leaving Mandy to quietly enjoy her Black Forest cake and laugh at their stories at the appropriate moments.

~~~

Mandy folded the paper and tossed it to the floor. As soon as she saw the elegant gold script on the box, she rationalized that her horoscope was abundantly clear on what she should do. She shrugged off any lingering guilt, took a quick sip of her glass of Merlot, and pounced on the box of assorted centers.

Easing the red satin ribbon over the corner, Mandy freed the box from its silky binding. Supporting the diagonal corners between her fingertips, she flicked her wrists to give the box two quick shakes. The momentary vibration was enough for the base to slide down out of the lid. She gazed at the dark velvety shapes nestled in their plastic form-fitting pockets and settled on the one that she knew she wanted the most. First gliding her fingertip over its gently curved, smooth surface, she then delicately removed the caramel center from its nest, crackling the plastic. Holding one end of the chocolate between her fingertips, Mandy slowly brought it up to her waiting lips. With the rich brown oval between her front teeth, Mandy tilted her head back, breaking the chocolate in half. The sticky sweet caramel ran over her lower lip. Embracing it in her mouth, the chocolate melted over her tongue and coated the caramel as the mixture slid down her throat.

~~~

Mandy had given Calvin a long, passionate kiss outside of

her apartment after their date. The kiss started tenderly—a mere goodnight kiss. As she gradually increased the pressure of her lips against his, she ran her fingers through his hair above the nape of his neck. She gently massaged and caressed the palm of his right hand while she leaned her body against his, pushing him towards the doorway. She squeezed his hand as she withdrew, both of them taking a deep breath in its wake.

"Why don't we go camping on the long weekend? Spend some time alone in the middle of nowhere." She arched her eyebrows as she smiled. "Could be fun. What do you think?"

"I wasn't planning on going away for the weekend."

"You were already making plans? Why didn't you mention it over dinner?"

His hand still in hers, Calvin followed Mandy into her apartment. "I've been inviting people over to a barbecue at my place Saturday afternoon and then to the Jays game."

"People?"

Calvin kicked off his shoes and settled himself on the sofa while Mandy disappeared into her bedroom. "The usual—Pete, Geoff, Jen and Dave, Libby. Steve might be in town."

"And?"

"And what? I haven't talked to anyone else. I don't want it to be a huge party or anything."

Mandy came back into the living room with her jacket removed, her shirt untucked and holding a hair brush. "Do you know what's right before the long weekend?" she asked.

"I know it's your birthday. A barbecue at my place would be fun to do for your birthday."

"Then why are you just inviting your friends?"

"They're your friends, too, aren't they? You can invite whoever you want."

"Are we at least doing something Friday night?"

"You know I have to have dinner with my family on Friday nights."

Mandy walked back into her bedroom. "You're mad at me," Calvin stated.

She returned to the living room with her hair brushed out and her shirt tucked back into her skirt. "Damn right I'm mad!"

"Why? What did I do?"

Mandy took a deep breath as she sat down on the sofa. She turned to face Calvin, but chose to study the fabric of the cushion between them for a moment. When she looked up, her eyes were no longer blazing with anger. "Why are you avoiding me?" she asked.

"I'm not avoiding you. We went out tonight. We've got plans for your birthday."

"You've got plans with your friends on the long weekend. You didn't even ask me."

"I told you about it now. I said you could invite whoever you want."

Mandy looked levelly at Calvin, trying to make eye contact. "We never spend time alone anymore."

Calvin turned from Mandy's direction and tried to find the remote control in amongst the newspapers on her coffee table. "I don't know why you always make such a big deal about it. It's not like we're married or anything."

Mandy snapped her head back. "Excuse me?"

"We were together twenty-four hours a day at school. You act as if we're married. We weren't and we aren't. We shouldn't be spending so much time together."

She snatched the remote control from him before he could turn on the TV. "So what are we?"

Still looking at the coffee table, Calvin took a deep breath before responding, "I'm very happy with you, Mandy, but it's not forever. Not now. I don't want to break up with you now. I just want some space and maybe...."

"Maybe what? Calvin, look at me. What do you want? Some space so you can find a replacement before you break up with me?"

"No! Nothing like that. It's just... I want... We're... I'm not ready for any serious commitment. I didn't plan on meeting someone like you so soon. I still want to sow my wild oats, so to speak. I need to play the field, have some fun. You know me–I always think that somewhere out there I could be having more fun than I'm having now."

"So I'm not fun? Is that it? I'm boring?"

"No!" Calvin turned to face Mandy and smiled wryly. "You're definitely not boring. It's just that...it's just that I need to know that women still look at me, like, they're attracted to me."

"You want to do the bar scene?"

"Sort of. Just play the field. Meet new people." Mandy held his gaze for a moment and saw something different in his eyes. "Let me get this straight. You *want* to go back to the dating game? From what you've told me, you spent a lot of time alone or drunk. Why would you want to do that?"

Calvin looked at the ceiling as he replied, "Because I need to. I need to try." He returned Mandy's level gaze. "My first love hit me like a thunderbolt. I love you, but it wasn't like that. I want to find that thunderbolt again."

Mandy swallowed hard and took a deep breath. She set her jaw and narrowed her eyes as she studied Calvin's face. He was still looking at her, taking in short breaths as if he was about to say something but then decided against it. His pale blue eyes shone with emotion. Mandy's face was an immovable mask staring at Calvin, her deep brown eyes searching for some explanation.

Calvin softly touched Mandy's cheek. "Please say something. I can't tell what you're thinking. Tell me!"

Several seconds passed before she coldly moved away from his hand and quietly said, "When you're ready to tell me the whole truth, give me a call."

~

Tilting her lips back toward the remaining bite of chocolate, Mandy swirled the tip of her tongue inside the hollow shell, drawing out the golden brown syrup. After slowly licking the caramel from her lips, she closed her eyes and slipped the semi-sweet shell into her mouth. As the rich creamy flavor washed to the back of her mouth, she leaned back into the sofa cushions, exhaling a deep breath of lingering pleasure.

After Calvin had left her apartment, Mandy packed up every picture, every gift, and nearly every reminder of her relationship with Calvin in a box, marked it "school," and put it in the back of her hall closet. On returning to the living room, she discovered that she had left two items next to the newspaper on her coffee table–the box of chocolates and the last of the Merlot she and Calvin had bottled. She had forgotten that she had taken out the wine for after their date. Deciding that she needed to be comfortable, Mandy wandered back into her bedroom to change into her track pants and a T-shirt.

~~~

Taking another sip of Merlot, Mandy perused the chocolate map and decided on her next conquest. She plucked out a dome and extracted the cherry with her first bite. She then snapped up a double chocolate mint and slowly bit through the rich, dense center with her front teeth, melting the chocolate in her mouth before swallowing. Chuckling at herself, she polished off a crisp toffee-center in two quick nibbles. The hazelnut cluster was finished off whole. One by one, Mandy popped each chocolate into her mouth, her smile widening. By the time she ate the last orange fondant, she couldn't stop giggling at what she was doing. After draining the last glass of wine to wash down the sugar, she sat back to look at the remains from the evening. She smiled.

Mandy roughly shoved the cork back into the empty bottle and crammed the lid onto the box. She dropped them neatly into the recycling bin in the kitchen on her way to bed for a sound night's sleep.

Wendy Lewis

Betrayal

Cars whizzed by, bluebirds squawked and she sat on. Despite the pain in her gut, she kept sitting.

"Why did you do this?" he said.

She listened to the dull rumble of traffic gradually coming to a crescendo as the cars approached and then faded away, one after another. It was a bright June morning, almost too bright, and she didn't want to think about words like betrayal, faithfulness and hope.

"I don't know," she answered, picking at her cuticle and noticing a car sounding a little like a jet taking off. The sun felt good on her shoulders, warm and comforting. She didn't want to think.

He tapped his fingers on the white enamel arm of the lawn chair impatiently. Clearly her response did not satisfy and he was waiting for more.

"Because I'm a bad person," she said, as if trying to guess the right answer. "Because I'm not trustworthy?" she asked.

He let out a long sigh. Suddenly she wanted to laugh–the tension seemed so needless, but she couldn't think of anything funny to say. Now she noticed a silence in the car sounds, a pause in the traffic.

He frowned at her and she knew he was not satisfied.

"What else could I do?" she asked, hoping to volley the ball back into his court. *Whoever speaks first loses,* she thought to herself, and there was a long pause. She took a deep breath and let it out slowly. A truck passed by, filling her head with a clatter and roar.

"Oh forget it," he said with a look of exasperation. "I'm going to the store to get another one, and I'm eating it before I get home."

He pushed up from the lawn chair and strutted off with an air of self-righteous indignation, and she neatly licked the last bits of chocolate éclair off her fingers and wiped her hands one last time on the crumpled napkin, smeared with chocolate and custard, in her lap.

Transitions

Barbara Lazarony

Black-Tie Optional

My father is a descendant of women penguins,
it's reflected in his gait.
He walks with his hands folded into his chest
and a slight waddle.
He's a dead ringer for a wind-up toy,
big foot over big foot.
He demonstrates this stride when he's nervous,
like the day he walked me down the aisle.
I was barely able to wedge my hand under his left armpit
as we began our ascent to the altar.
One big step, body pitched to the right;
another big step, body pitched to the left,
and so it continued.
By the time we reached my awaiting groom
my dress was soiled from the chaotic brush of flowers
and the skin between my thighs began to smart;
two raw slabs of flesh already spent for their
honeymoon night.

Barbara Lazarony

Sawmill

empty
hollow
barren

void of promise, hope, joy

    bottomless
    downward
    spiraling

    void of promise, hope, joy

        expired
        expelled
        ostracized

        void of promise, hope, joy

carpenter ants attempting to hitch a ride on a
    pure,
    wholesome,
    virginal

    piece of wood that has tumbled into a stream
        a stream   that opens unto a river,
                      that opens unto a holding lake,
                      that opens unto a sawmill
                      that opens unto a diamond cut blade.

Eileen McLaughlin

A Moment

It was just a few pieces of paper,
a bit of accounting.
Nothing more.

The woman,
back bent below curls of gray-white,
it was she who turned away,
face to the ground,
voice barely acknowledging
her own error.

Eighty and more years
of independence, of competence,
crashing down
in a moment, a flash of clarity.

Her own child,
purveyor of truth,
wordless as witness and villain.

Barbara Lazarony

Lighthouse

She had worked all her life to be perfect,
the perfect daughter,
the perfect student,
the perfect dresser,
the perfect athlete,
the perfect woman working in a man's world.

She did it all because she believed she had to,
she had to do it for herself and for her parents,
for the other women and even for the men.
This was her role, she believed, for 23 hours a day.

But that last hour was her time to write,
to pour out her heart onto the pages of her journal,
the pages pressed between the most perfect pink binding
    you've ever seen.

And she would write.
And she would write.
And she would write.

About her knobby knees,
and her second toe that was much larger than her first,
and spelling words she still couldn't get right years later,
and math equations she couldn't solve,
and about the clothes without labels from being bought at
    the discount store,
and her lack of desire to get out of bed to go to the gym,
and her utter distaste for competition,
and the hours she needed to keep being "one of the boys,"
and the things she had to say,

and the feelings she needed to squash down.
Clutching her journal with all of her life, she asked in the dark silence of 3 a.m.:

"How does that story go?"

"The commanding vessel cut through the rough ocean water, running with all its knowledge and experience toward port, coming upon a light in the deep darkness of night, it signaled,
 'I am the mighty vessel, turn immediately, and let me pass.'
The responding light answered,
 'Turn away!'
The vessel signaled again,
 'I am the mighty vessel, turn immediately or I will be forced to ram you.'
The responding light said with ultimate strength and feeling,
 'Turn away, I am the lighthouse!'"

Wendy Lewis

Courage

I didn't expect to discover a joy
in dragging the garbage carts on their wheels
over the unpaved drive,
in the pitch black night,
even in the rain.

Because it was my trash,
and not a man's job,
the dogs bounding ahead
like joyous guardians
quick to bark at snapping twigs
and rustlings in the dark.

My heart is strong and with me
as the cans bump along,
even on a wild night
with the road full of fallen branches and stones.

My face flushes in the night air
and fine drops settle in my hair
making it curl,
and I untie my boots by the doorway,
oddly satisfied.

Wendy Lewis

Cancer

Under stress, your immune system malfunctions
and one cell of cancer can get through.

She thought of that, and remembered when he hit her.
She remembered her heart, pounding so hard
that she could see the jump of it through her coat.
Flailing with outrage and fury,
abandoned and lost in the dark.

He said he didn't really hit her.
Standing on the stairway she showed him her face,
crimson on one side, white on the other.

And when he told her he was leaving,
her body shook and her teeth chattered.
She was cold and reeling,
lost in waves that wouldn't stop.
Drowning, falling, cursing in silent screams.
Wanting to smash windows.
Begging for a warm touch and tender kiss.
Lost, alone and broken.

Now she knows,
those were the moments
when the cancer cell got through.
It multiplied when all her troops
were rallied against the loss.
Defenses wasted on injustice and fury,
followed by defeat, regret and pain.

Now she mourns and tries to heal
from cancer and from a broken heart.

Wendy Lewis

Recovery

I want to write about fragrant spring days
and going for short walks
because I'm delicate
and need to heal.

What will make me stronger?
What will cause an accumulation of fluids?
What will cause excessive strain?

I want to run and shout
and find the perfect man
to touch my body.

I want someone to know exactly
which secret places
make me moan
and fill with pleasure.

I don't want to compromise
or to be careful.
I don't want to hurry.

I am learning patience,
and I feel solid and connected,
knowing I will die
and hoping not for a long time.
Knowing I am flawed
but discovering perfection
at the same time.

Maybe my wounds are perfect
and my disability a gift,
somehow.
And I am patient
and waiting to open the package
to find the sparkling jewels
that really were there all along.

Wendy Lewis

The Raft

I've paddled so hard,
sweating, developing blisters
where the oars rub against the base of my thumbs.
I've gotten out and kicked till I was breathless,
thinking I would be more powerful in the water.

I've cried.
I've called out in panic.
I've begged for help.
And still, the river propelled me
in a direction I didn't want to go.

I barely missed being dashed
against boulders.
I ducked my head
to avoid sharp branches
that scratched my back and shoulders.

But finally the water calms.
I still have not reached the far bank,
but I know that when I get there,
and where I wash up to shore
will be the perfect time and place.

I know that warm hands will reach out
to pull me from the raft.
And I'll be held and comforted
and fed exquisite morsels,
French cheeses and reddish-black cherries
that burst with juice when I bite into them.

The Raft / Wendy Lewis

I'm tired of rowing with all my might.
My arms are sore and my chest aches.
So I lie flat and let the breeze waft over my face.
I bake in the warm sun and feel my breath.

I split a section of wood from the raft
and form a rudder.
Slowly I guide myself
toward the solid ground
of the far bank,
barely visible in the distance.

I take my time,
because I know that I will get there.
I hear the birds singing sweetly.
Cool water splashes my feet.
I listen to the trickle and rush
of the whirlpools and eddies,
and I know that I will
get there at just the right time.

Traci Post

Fear

War and terror
Acts of inhumane brutality
There's peace to be had,
but not by our world,
not today.
The uncertainty.

Never having a child
Not knowing what I missed.
The emptiness.

Walking alone in a dark parking garage,
shadows jumping and
heat from behind.
The unwanted attention.

A bathroom shower curtain
Closed. I can't see behind it.
The unknown.

Floating face down
in the salty Caribbean sea,
eyes and nose masked.
Down below, in another world,
a gray shark dances with her baby.
The unpredictable.

Plugging in a hair dryer
Dog's water dish below.
Don't drop it, not there.
Anywhere but there.
The irrational.

My aging mother's forgetfulness,
not the past, the present.
Time's heartless erosion of brain, body, spirit
into a dark sea.
The inevitable.

Life's challenges:
See them approach,
Watch them creep closer,
must act
paralysis strikes.
Fear.

Liza Wood

Sloe Dog

It felt strange for Beth to sit at the bar instead of her usual table. By herself and with nothing to read, she scrutinized the snack menu left by the previous occupant of her seat. She was only slightly tempted to browse the web on her Linq, but she didn't care to read the latest tech news.

"You're PurpleEng421 at Netlink, right?" The bartender checked his tablet as he placed a coaster in front of Beth. "A bunch of people came in at once. Just making sure I'm matching the right person with the network link."

"That's me."

"Want the usual?"

"Do you know how to make an old-fashioned?"

"Don't get many requests for those. No problem. I'll look it up."

With a subtle flourish, the bartender tapped on his tablet as he found his way to a cocktail reference guide on the web. "Ah-ha! One old-fashioned coming right up."

Beth gave a slight nod of appreciation. As she watched him select the liquors from the bank of bottles behind him, Beth realized that she had never really noticed him before. He was quite good-looking in a non-spectacular sort of way. Trying to be inconspicuous, Beth tilted her head as he bent over to retrieve a bottle of bitters from the bottom shelf.

Feeling a bit self-conscious, she slid her Linq off her left wrist and pretended to study it in her hands. She could have bought a Linq that was more like an old fashioned wrist watch. It would have been more practical. It was a moment of whimsy when she bought the bangle bracelet Linq. She liked the smooth brown plastic and gold trim around the inch-square touch-screen. The holographic projector just above the screen, disguised to look like a topaz gemstone set into the plastic, sparkled in the halogen lights hanging above the bar.

When she slipped it over her hand every morning, it felt more like she was putting on jewelry rather than a link to the Internet.

"So, PurpleEng421, do you have a real name?"

"Beth."

"Hi, Beth. I'm Jim. Are you a multi-millionaire or completely ruined? Your stocks. That's what you're watching there, isn't it?

Beth sighed and put her Linq on the bar. "No. Not tonight. I guess a lot of people do that here."

"Yeah, but you're usually at the corner table surrounded by your work or reading the business news. You never come up for air."

Beth studied his face for a moment before answering. "I do that, don't I?"

"Mind if I ask you something?"

"Sure, why not."

"Why do you always order a gin and lime? Never a Tom Collins. Gin and lime. My new servers get confused."

Beth smiled. "I don't like the soda. Besides, don't you charge a dollar more for two cents worth of bubbles?"

"Secret of the trade." He grinned and dropped a cherry in her glass.

"Here you go. One old-fashioned."

As Beth picked up her glass, her Linq made a slight buzz and skittered across the bar. Still holding her glass in her right hand, she caught her bracelet in her left. With her index finger, she tapped an acknowledgement on its screen as she downed half her drink with a quick twist of her wrist. A second later, her face pinched and she shook her head.

"If you don't like the soda, then why did you order an old-fashioned?"

Beth plucked the cherry from her glass, snapped off the stem between her front teeth, held in her mouth for a second before eating it. "I wanted something bitter," she mumbled between chews.

Jim took the half empty glass off the bar. "I'll make you something I think you'll like better."

"You don't have to."

"The old-fashioned was on the house."

"Thanks." Beth looked down the bar.

Trying to appear casual, she slowly turned to face the room, her right elbow still resting on the bar. Even for a Monday night, the place was quiet. The after-work crowd had gone home over an hour ago. Beth had arrived at the same time as a group of college interns, who were now sitting in the largest booth at the back, chatting about the weekend's escapades over a pitcher of beer. An elderly man was sitting at Beth's usual corner table by the door, reading something on his tablet and nursing a snifter of cognac. He hadn't even bothered to take off his coat. As she observed this man, Beth noticed a couple, about her age, walk by the window. They were holding hands but the man, still with his corporate ID badge around his neck, was talking on his cell phone. The woman looked through the plate glass window into the bar as they walked by.

"Try this."

Beth turned to face Jim and saw a pale cocktail in a squat glass on the bar in front of her. She picked it up and took a tentative sip. It tasted sour, but the aftertaste was bitter. "Not bad. What is it?"

"It's called Sloe Dog. Gin with grapefruit juice, but I get to charge you a buck extra." He winked. "I found it on the same site as the old-fashioned."

As she took a second sip, her Linq buzzed again. This time it fell in her lap before she managed to catch it. Placing her drink back down on the bar, she tapped an acknowledgement and put the bracelet next to her drink.

"Aren't you going to answer that?"

"Why should I?"

"Someone could be trying to get a hold of you."

"Like who?"

"I don't know. Significant Other? Stockbroker? Work?"

"It's probably just you. I set it to buzz whenever something is charged to my account."

"But I didn't charge you for the last one."

Beth tilted her Linq slightly to glance at the display. She gave a wry smile as she dropped it back on the bar. "Another one of these," she pointed to her half-empty glass.

"Stocks take a dive again in after-hours trading?"

Beth dismissed that question with a wave of her hand. "My stocks have been under water for months. They're all long-term investments now." The other half of her drink was gone. "That's just what I need now–long term investments," she scoffed.

Jim replaced her empty glass with a fresh cocktail. Before her Linq had a chance to buzz again, Beth silenced it with a couple of quick taps. Starting to feel the warmth of the gin radiate through her, Beth only took a small sip to savor the sour-bitter. She stared at the glass, running her index finger along the smooth upper edge. She waited for Jim to return to the bar after clearing the interns' recently vacated table.

"Have you ever thought about unplugging?" she asked him.

"I put my Linq in privacy mode when I need it."

"No. I mean being completely unplugged–off the network. No Linq. No tablets. Nothing."

"You're kidding, right?"

"No."

Jim pulled two brown mugs from under the bar, filled them both with coffee, and slid one between Beth and her Sloe Dog.

Beth ignored the gesture. "I'm dead serious and still quite sober. Have you ever wondered what it would be like to be completely off the network?"

Jim set his mug down behind the bar. He picked up a freshly washed wine goblet and began to dry it. "How would you live? We don't have cash or credit cards anymore. It's all network transactions."

Beth sipped her Sloe Dog and considered that for a moment.

"Barter," she responded.

"What about communications?"

"What about communications?" she answered. "I still have a phone."

"Which has an IP address. It may be a phone but it is part of the network."

"Hmmm. Good point. I guess the phone would have to be unplugged, too."

"Why not just use privacy mode? Or turn it off when you want to be alone? I don't see what the difference is."

"People can leave messages. There's an expectation for you to respond. Hell, people from work will call, expecting an answer–even if you don't work for the damn company anymore."

Jim hung the polished wine goblet upside down in the rack above his head. He picked up another glass and began to wipe it.

Beth pushed the coffee mug aside. She picked up the stronger beverage and brought the glass to her lips, but then put it back on the bar. "If you're disconnected from the network, you don't exist. No porch light. No one's home. There are no expectations because you can't be reached."

Jim looked at Beth for a moment, trying to make eye contact. She stared at the low ball between her hands as if the gin and grapefruit juice were showing her fortune.

"So it was today." He hung the glass in the rack.

"Do you always ask so many questions?" There was an edge to Beth's voice. She sighed. "Sorry."

"A bartender hears things. I read the announcement of impending layoffs on the news sites. A lot of people in here mentioned it would be happening soon."

"I didn't seriously think I'd be one of them, you know?" Beth's voice shook for a second. She sipped her drink. "All month we speculated on who it would be. Bottom five percent–they were easy to pick out. We all felt pretty generous towards them because at least they were getting a better package this way. The old timers could retire. Still, that wouldn't make the numbers. Numbers. Ten years–how's that for a number? Did you know the average person only stays at the same company for five years? I had different jobs–even got promoted–every couple of years but had no reason to jump ship. I guess I should have."

Beth pointed at the empty glass she had put down in front of her. Jim pushed the coffee back towards her. She pushed the coffee away from Jim's reach and the empty glass toward him. He shrugged and began refilling it.

Beth drank her Sloe Dog in silence. The bar was empty now, except for Beth and the old man, still in his coat. Jim started closing up.

With a tilt of her head, Beth took the last gulp of her drink and set the empty glass next to the now cold coffee mug. She rummaged through the pockets of her coat hung over the stool next to her and extracted a silver pen. She ran her thumb over the engraving of her initials. Pens were rare gifts these days. Beth snatched a cocktail napkin from a stack at the end of the bar. She smiled and scribbled on the napkin.

After Beth slipped her Linq back on her wrist and put on her coat, she called out to Jim, who was sweeping the floor by the back booth. "Hey, Jim. I don't normally do this... but...phone me sometime." She lifted the cocktail napkin and dropped it back on the bar.

"Let me call you a cab."

"No worries. I'll flag one outside."

When the crisp night air hit Beth's face, she decided to walk. In these hours between last call and the early morning commuters, the streets and sidewalks were calm but not empty. As she walked home, she stopped in front of the building where she had spent most of the past ten years. The lobby lights were dimmed. A young security guard was at the reception desk, fighting off sleep. He straightened when he saw Beth and nodded a greeting. Beth returned the nod and regarded the company logo emblazoned on the wall behind him. The silver lines rose and fell, rose and fell. Beth smiled for the first time that day. She felt content for the first time in many years.

Beth's one bedroom condo was only a few blocks farther. As usual, it was dark and empty when she entered. Closing the door behind her, she leaned against it and surveyed her residence. Even in the shadows of the city night, Beth could see the picture from her college days outlined on the top of a bookshelf. In her mind's eye she could see the picture clearly. Beth was with her best college friends, her skin dyed completely purple, partying on a rival school's football field after her school's victory.

She sighed and walked into the kitchen, freeing her hair from its clip. Leaving the clip on the counter, she opened her freezer and removed the only item in it–double chocolate fudge ice cream. Still in darkness, she plucked a spoon from the drying rack next to the sink. She carried the ice cream and spoon out to the balcony and left them on the table.

Wandering back inside, Beth pulled the fuzzy black throw blanket off her sofa and the cushion off the wooden chair by the door. Back on the balcony, she snapped the lid off the ice cream and plunged the spoon into it. After licking the spoon clean from her first taste of chocolate decadence, Beth slipped her Linq from her wrist. Two taps on its face and it was in full vibrate mode, capable of politely alerting her to any messages. Beth leaned over the railing and grinned when she saw the sidewalk five floors below. She perched her Linq on top of the railing.

Beth settled into her patio chair, the cushion protecting her from the chill of the cold plastic. Warmly wrapped in the throw blanket, she savored every spoon of ice cream and gazed at the stars. They're beautiful stars, she thought as she waited for someone to buzz.

Broken Windows, Empty Hallways

The stale, heavy air of August hung lifelessly around Hazel Puffkin. She perched on dry elbows at the limestone kitchen counter, working the crossword puzzle in the five-week-old *TV Guide*. She searched her mind for the answer to nine-down - "The Star of Starsky & Hutch" - while absently struggling for air. She traded her pen for her cigarette and managed a shallow inhalation of familiar tangy smoke from her Virginia Slims, the ashes glowing orange as they burnt to the filter. She pushed the smoldering tip into the overflowing ashtray. Hazel reached for the green and white pack lying between her glass of iced tea and potato chips. She tapped it against the stone only to find it empty. Sitting up straight she opened the drawer under the counter where she kept her supply. The drawer was empty, too. There must be more somewhere. She moved on to search her secret hiding spots where she kept her "emergency stash." She rummaged through the cluttered counter drawers, pulling out dusty kitchen utensils, hotel pens, paper clips, and coupons until she uncovered her last pack of smokes.

Before she could unwrap the cellophane, her body convulsed with a phlegmy cough, her mind black as she struggled to pull air into her lungs. She reached for her tea and choked down the cool liquid until her glass was empty. She stumbled to the refrigerator to fill her cup with ice and filtered water from the built-in machine. The water soothed and moistened her dry throat, quieting the cough enough so she could remove the thin gold band of cellophane and ease out a fresh smoke. She lit her cigarette with a *Happy Heifer Steak House* match.

The smoke filled her mouth and flowed down her throat, where it was quickly rejected by her congested lungs. Her face flushed with blood and heat as she coughed the smoke out into the kitchen air.

Perched at the counter, Hazel settled in again to continue work on the puzzle, alternating pen for cigarette in a well-practiced rhythm. Stubborn as a Mexican mule under a shady tree, she'd refused to see old Doc Webber at the small clinic up on Pine Street for a check up. Her three-pack-a-day habit for four decades had her lungs more accustomed to cigarette smoke than plain ol' suburban air. Smoking was her hobby. The nicotine-laced smoke filled her with pleasure, feeding her insatiable craving only to leave her wanting more, like a good lover.

It was this constant quest for fulfillment that delivered her to death's door that sticky August day. But luckily for her, death did not answer the insistent knock as her lungs were taken over by fluid, squeezing at the chambers of her heart while she worked the *TV Guide* crossword puzzle, dozing uncontrollably as her mind and body were deprived of oxygen.

~~~

Hazel's husband, Robert, unfolded his long legs from his Chrysler Le Baron and stepped onto the paved driveway. He had a break in his day from interviewing prospective buyers of the Fairwaters' sprawling ranch home on Mountain Vista Drive. Hazel was on his mind. He was afraid her damn cold was only getting worse, and she refused to quit smoking. In all their years of marriage, he had witnessed each and every one of her failed attempts to quit.

He shifted the bag of groceries resting on his hip and pressed the brass latch to open the wide oak door. He'd picked up some Vitamin C tablets, Sunshine Orange Juice and a box of Mrs. Grass's Chicken Noodle Soup with the golden egg. Robert's baritone voice echoed in the entryway when he called out Hazel's name. He found her with her head on the kitchen counter, cigarette burnt to the stub in the curve of the ashtray.

Robert lifted her head and noticed the blue tint of her lips and nose. He grabbed her shoulders and shook her until she woke gagging and coughing.

"Can you stand up?" he asked, wrapping an arm around her, lifting her out of the cushioned seat.

"What the hell do you want? Leave me alone. I'm fine."

"You're not fine. I'm taking you to the hospital."

"Like hell you are!" Her head rolled forward, eyes closed.

Robert lifted her and carried her to his car. Tucking her into the small black leather bucket seat, he ignored the seat belt and ran around to the driver's side.

Reversing down the driveway, Robert sped past Kelly's Corner Market, Benson's Furniture Store and Pete's Gas Mart, dialing the hospital to tell them he was on his way with his very sick wife. He ignored the friendly wave from the Hutchinsons as they meandered through the park. With a rush of air he let go of the breath he'd been holding and pulled his car into the tree-lined emergency room carport of Crest View Hospital.

Two nurses, one large and one skinny, met him with a wheelchair. The pale rotund nurse fired question after question at Robert: the patient's name, age, drugs she was using, medical history. Hazel was wheeled through the beige corridor into a room enclosed by a faded striped curtain. Robert recognized Dr. John Tallac, tanned smile-wrinkles at the corners of his eyes. The two shook hands, ignoring the bad blood that had festered between them since high school, when they had fought over Hazel. Dr. Tallac issued orders to the nurses, calling for oxygen, vitals, and the portable x-ray machine. He turned to Robert and asked him to step outside. Robert overheard Dr. Tallac comment to Alice Ready, the skinny redhead nurse: "Hazel Puffkin is as close to dead as they come."

~~~

When Hazel returned home from the hospital, her youngest daughter, Sonia, came to stay with her for a few weeks. Sonia, married for three years, had no children and no job other than playing tennis at the club three times a week, and golf on Thursdays. Her husband, Rich, ran a financial services business in the City. While staying with Hazel, Sonia arranged for Mary Beth Perkins, owner of Tidy Homes, to come clean the house twice a week, and for Mr. Peterson from the ambulatory supply store to bring fresh canisters of oxygen and enough silvery-white tubing to run throughout the house so Hazel could walk from one end of the first level to the other without having to move the canister of oxygen. The doctors were hopeful that after a month of being on oxygen twenty-four hours a day, Hazel would be able to move around without being tethered to the oxygen tank. Sadly, there was no hope of undoing the brain damage caused from the extended period she went without oxygen while she was sick.

Hazel frequently asked Sonia to explain the events surrounding her hospital stay. She had no recollection of being sick or of going to the hospital. The doctors said the memory loss was a potentially short-term side effect.

The best part of Hazel's stint in the hospital was that she went through the tortuous process of withdrawal from cigarettes. Her brush with death left her wanting more: more from her life, her marriage, and herself. The reality of just how completely empty her life had become was abundantly clear.

She was the retired mother of three daughters who were all grown and independent, and she had not done anything meaningful since the birth of her youngest child. Clara and Beth lived in the City and rarely came home because of their busy social schedules. But her beautiful baby Sonia still lived in town, although she, too, rarely visited until after Hazel got sick.

Hazel had been married for thirty-three years, and there wasn't a day that went by now that was not only vaguely familiar, but identical to the hundreds of days before. The truth was that Hazel Puffkin was bored to death. And now without the pleasure that smoking granted her, the tedium of her daily activities were hollow and suffocating.

She couldn't remember where she had put things and was easily irritated. The crossword puzzles that she had loved so much were dull, and she had absolutely no interest in playing bridge with the ladies at the River Foundation. She wished like hell that Robert wouldn't work so much. She wanted his company, but he wouldn't change his habits and worked until eight, sometimes nine o'clock at night.

It helped having Sonia around at first, and it was quite entertaining the first few days as they looked through photo albums and reminisced about their younger days. But the daily routine settled in: she woke at 6:00 a.m., ground fresh French Roast beans, sipped her cup of coffee at the counter and flipped through the morning paper, only to wonder how she would spend the next ten hours before Robert came home. The market or the mall? Cards or a long drive? She found it difficult to remember how she used to spend her time before becoming sick and wondered if she'd smoked her days away doing nothing.

After fourteen days Hazel craved her space, her freedom to do exactly what she chose, catching up on her soap opera instead of the trashy talk shows Sonia was into. By the end of her second week at home, Hazel suggested to Sonia that she should move back with Rich, that she was indeed able to care for herself now.

Sonia appeared happy to oblige. Between worrying sick over her mother while she was in the hospital and watching over her at home, Sonia also yearned for her own routine.

She left on Saturday morning. Robert and Hazel stood on the porch waving goodbye as their baby girl sped her sporty blue car down the street. Mr. and Mrs. Hutchinson hurried by and shouted their greeting, chasing after their golden-brown cocker spaniel, Tidbit. Before Sonia's car was out of sight, Robert announced he was going to work and asked Hazel if she needed anything before he left.

With the house to herself, Hazel went in search of her smokes. She no longer craved them. Not anymore. But she just wanted to make sure they were all gone. Just in case she had a moment of weakness at some point down the road.

She sifted through the contents of the counter drawers, the bottom of the china hutch, the back of the kitchen towel drawer, the cupboard beneath her bathroom sink, and the top pantry shelves, where she found the sole pack of Dunhills.

She hadn't smoked a Dunhill since she quit playing bridge on Monday mornings. The women would look admiringly at her pack every week. It was not likely they knew she saved them for the bridge match and smoked the cheapest cigarettes in the privacy of her own home when no one else was looking. Hazel could not recall where her other hiding places were. Perhaps it was the short-term memory loss. *Yes. That was it.*

~~~

Hazel Puffkin did not remember ever not knowing her daughter. Twenty-six years ago she had felt the dance her daughter performed in her belly during the last three months of her pregnancy. She knew the pitch of her little girl's first wail as she welcomed the new world, reluctantly saying goodbye to her safe cocoon. She could vividly recall her girl's first steps at Sunshine Nursery, the appearance of her first tooth at Rockwell's Family Restaurant, the sound of her first word "dog," at Spring Valley Park, and the first time she said "bless you" when Hazel sneezed. Those were the memories that made a mother's life worth living.

But today, five months after her near-death experience when her daughter had stood at her bedside and prayed ferociously as only a good Protestant girl could, Hazel experienced a frightening moment of forgetfulness. A "senior moment," she assured herself, but all the same, she could not recall her youngest girl's name.

The girl with the tanned face and full lips and high cheekbones came to mind, and how she looked with metal braces over her small teeth when she was ten. It was a vivid memory, as were the solid 9.8 scores from her gymnastic championships. "Chuckles" was the name of her raggedy stuffed teddy bear who had sat on her pink bedspread until she moved out two years ago. All of these memories were clear, but not her daughter's name.

She needed to do something. The pantry was the closest thing to attack, so for the third time that week, Hazel Puffkin rearranged the contents of her pantry, with absolutely no recollection that she had done it just five hours earlier.

The disease consumed Hazel's brain, propelling her into a deep darkness, her soul suffocated by the absence of memory. Mugged of her past and her present, she didn't understand that she now lived at a convalescent home twenty miles from her real home. The home where she raised her children, cooked wonderful meals, and sewed Barbie clothes for her girls was only a vague memory that flittered around the edges of her consciousness. She no longer had the clarity to understand that this was her new home, and would be so for the remainder of her illness and life. The contents of her world were emptied upon the soil of time, eroded by the savage beast that steals, tricks and lies to her.

Who's this girl? Hazel wondered silently looking at the woman standing beside her chair. She seemed nervous and kept shifting her weight from one sling-back pump to the other, her hands twirling the gold key ring nervously around her white-tipped fingers. She was saying something, but Hazel didn't really listen and waited patiently for the woman to leave. Instead of leaving, the woman sat down across from Hazel, her black linen suit whispering as she crossed her legs and then her arms. The woman grabbed the hand of the older gentleman standing beside her chair.

"Mom, it's me, Sonia. And Dad? Remember us?"

Sheila? No, that's not it. Oh what the hell. Children? Whose children is she speaking of? And a dog? I don't have a dog. She's crazy talking to me, a total stranger, about her dog.

Sheila? That was the name of my dog. Sheila. Yes. That was it. She had a blue eye and a brown eye that had just a fleck of blue along the top rim. She would chase the Westchesters' tabby cat across the bluegrass lawn and through the hedge that separated our property.

This woman is my daughter? Oh, she's talking nonsense now.

I never had a daughter. Never wanted children really. No husband, no children, no pets. Just a free woman who could do as I please, travel all around the world to lands far, far away. That was me.

The poor woman must be lonely. She just needs someone to talk

to. Perhaps she'll stay for dinner. I could bake my famous pineapple downside up cake. Upside down? Downside up? Pineapple, flour, sugar, Karo syrup, mushrooms, Swiss Miss mocha...prime rib. I had prime rib last night. It was delicious.
"Delicious, I say. Absolutely delicious." Hazel finally spoke.
"What's delicious?" Sonia asked, leaning closer.
"Why it was perfectly tender, and ripe too. Absolutely ripe."
Like the prime rib we use to grill on the rotisserie on the giant black Webber BBQ in our backyard. We'd invite the Petersons. Good family. Nice boys who played so nicely with my girls.
Prime rib like we used to grill on the Webber. BBQ. Frosty mugs.
"How is your crossword puzzle going?" Sonia asked.
Hazel, suddenly furious, yelled, "I DON'T DO PUZZLES! DON'T ASK ME! You're nothing but applesauce. Applesauce, I tell you!"
Sonia sat back in her chair and stared beyond the large windows out to the fog that danced along the amber meadow. Hazel shuffled the papers, puzzle books and cards on her table, irritated as hell with these people.
"We had coleslaw for breakfast this morning. I tell you, ain't that wrong? Coleslaw. And prime rib for dinner. The chef is excellent here. The restaurant is open 24 hours a day. I could order me up a shrimp cocktail if I wanted. Uh huh. Shrimp cockatoo."
"Mom, it's me, Sonia. Can you just look at me for a few minutes and tell me you know who I am?" She leaned forward again, tears swimming behind the jet-black mascara barrier. "Please tell me you know who I am."
Flowers sure are perty this time of year. I think I'll grab me a Dunhill and sit outside and have me a smoke.
Why in heaven's name is this girl all bleary-faced?
Oh, sad thing she is. Her momma's not doing well, I hear. Cancer, I hear. Poor lass.
Maybe I'll have myself some tea. Yes. How delightful that will be. Tea. For two. And two for tea. And...Why that's Clara! When did she get here?
"Clara dear! How nice of you to come." The light in Hazel's eye turned on as she recognized her oldest daughter.

But she did not recognize the man with her, although there was something familiar about him.

"Are you my son?"

"No dear, it's me, Robert." His eyes welled with tears, and he looked out the window again as he saw no light of recognition, no sign at all that she knew who he was, just like every other time he visited.

"Mom? I'm Sonia. Not Clara. Remember, Clara's got dark hair? Two years older. Remember? I'm Sonia. Little Baby Sonia. 'Hell-on-wheels Sonia' you used to call me. Do you remember?"

"No. No, honey, you're Clara. But that's okay if you're a little confused. Go wash your hands, daddy will be home for dinner in a few minutes."

~~~

Hours later, visitors gone, Hazel Puffkin escaped. She wandered out during dinner. Terrible peas with gravy and sticky mashed potatoes. She longed for a puff on a nice Dunhill, so much so that she risked everything. Grabbing a coat from a nearby chair, she sneaked out the side door. Kelly's Corner Market was only a few blocks from her home. She could hit the market and be home before Clara knew she was gone. And Robert, too. He didn't have to know she still smoked.

Oblivious to cars and traffic, Hazel Puffkin stepped off the curb on the corner of Shadybrook and Meadow, directly in front of a Metro Bus going for the yellow light. As her body rolled under the wheels, witnesses on the sidewalk gasped as her slippers flew off, one onto the sidewalk, the other into the muddy gutter. Hazel's lifeless body came to rest just below the advertisement on the side of the bus. The colorful photo of a rugged cowboy on the back of a horse gazed down at Hazel, cowboy hat tilted to shade his eyes, a cigarette dangling from his weathered lips.

Eileen McLaughlin

I Cry

I cry.
Eyes aching,
gut tight, raw.
Heart empty.
Soul chaotic.

I cry.
Child anguished,
nights restless,
emotions drained.
When better?

I cry.
Danger close
to one of mine.
Safe, yes, and
fearful.

I cry.
Routines no more.
Now check, double-check.
Terror managed,
not denied.

I cry.
Mom's hometown
assaulted.
Roots violated.
Years melt to now.

I cry.
In print, familiar

name, death listed.
Acquaintance awoken
only to crash.

I cry.
Prayer in a crowd,
all faiths,
one green lawn.
Ends too soon.

I cry.
Childhood pal
promoted.
Sad, empty, joyless;
predecessor dead.

I cry.
Heroes and heroes
gone.
Never to know honor;
only tears remain.

I cry.
Naïveté, innocence
insulted.
Culture, country
stripped, exposed, naked.

I cry.
CNN sighted,
small boys exult our terror.
Youth so damaged,
born on blood-let streets.

I cry.
Ignorance abounding.
Citizens hunt
for color, country, belief,
as does the enemy.

I cry.
Patriotism broadcast,
blind, unthinking.
Glory of tolerance
invisible.

I cry.
Flag waves,
neighbor's house.
Gun-owner, NRA.
Walk quickly away.

I cry
in open space.
Chorus of quail and jay
meld with whine
of fighter jet.

I cry.
Life now unknown,
plans, path, purpose.
Struggle with my soul.
What is right?

I cry.

Living & Writing

Barbara Lazarony

The Backyard

Year 1 - An awkward, sloped drainage ditch encircles the property

Year 2 - Hand shoveled gravel forms the base, then black plastic laid down; the addition of a flagstone patio; sod laid between each stone and the open space

Year 3 - More greenery fills the landscape, koi pond added and even fish enjoy their new home

Year 4 - Some things die, others take hold; more greenery added; the trees are trimmed for the first time

Year 5 - The swing shows signs of rot and a new one is put in its place; the lilacs bloom for the first time

Year 6 - The sprinklers are too low, new ones are added to reach over the plants that are growing well

Year 7 - A new coat of yellow paint on the house is the perfect backdrop for an ever blooming yard of green, purple and white

Year 8 - Five baby kittens are born under the rose bush, they frolic and play on the trellis

Year 9 - The fish disappear, we determine it was a result of the big cranes we saw swooping

The Backyard / *Barbara Lazarony*

Year 10 - Cancerously overgrown,
    in dire need of attention,
      but still the best on the block.

The foundation's good,
    the roots are hearty, it's just...

    it needs tending,
      radiation and
        a hearty October breeze.

Betsy Gilliland

A Few Impressions of Uzbekistan, So I Don't Forget

The wrinkled white-beard man
in a worn chopon and telpak
grazing his sheep (and a goat)
in the grass
in the middle of the tracks
of the amusement park train.

The old woman
with one silver tooth
and the rest all rotted away
who talked to me in the post office
and was so happy to meet me.

The skinny young guy
working at the café in the entrance
to the university
who made me a cheese and salad sandwich
then microwaved it
so the cheese would melt.

The old Jewish woman
who sells seeds on the street
who asked me
if I was from Israel
and now calls me *dochka*
whenever I greet her.

The Korean women
at the bazaar
wearing floral aprons and head scarves
who let me taste every kind of salad

then don't complain
if I buy someone else's.

The plump woman at the Intourist desk
at the Tashkent airport
who was so nice to me
when everything else was going
very wrong.

The taxi drivers
at Bukhara airport
who know exactly where I live
and claim me
before I've even left the terminal
to take me home to my mud-walled house,
my sheep, and my host family who await me.

Wendy Lewis

The Winter

How soon will the long winter nights
give way to fuzzy yellow chicks
and fat buds on pussy willow branches?

I want to hold the darkness
and keep it close.
I want to rest in the quiet,
reflections on the wet sidewalk,
the moon alone in a cold sky.

Can I train my heart not to leap
at the brightness of the day,
with hope for brilliance,
wealth and flowers?

Can I welcome the gray
of the afternoon sky
that in summer comes much later?

Why do I still yearn for
magic, mystery, and surprises,
that a beauty that I've never seen before
is just around the corner?

That the sunset will flare
on the horizon with shades
of magenta and ochre, more
vivid than I've ever seen before.

That my heart will flood with
light and warmth and truth.
That it will be perfect
and that it will be enough.

Wendy Lewis

Turtle Faith

I am sitting solid
like a mountain or a tree.
Inert.

Ready to press forward,
one webbed foot
in front of the other
with little scratchy toes.

I've been knocked over
on my shell,
and spun around,
feet churning helplessly.
But now I'm turned back over,
and slowly making my way.

I'm the turtle looking for a
bit of water,
traveling inch by inch
over miles of hot sand.

I pull in my head and feet when
it's too hot to go on,
or when I'm afraid,
with a shadow looming over me.

I'm a stone,
blending into the desert sand.
No one knows my name.

Sometimes there is a trickle
of a stream

and leafy shade,
and I rest a long, long time.

I bathe in the coolness.
My tongue snatches at gnats
and mosquitoes.
I rest.

Then I trudge forward,
inch by inch,
trusting instinct,
guided by faith
one webbed foot
in front of the other,
going the only way there is.

Barbara Lazarony

Why I Write Poetry

I write for me, no one else, but for me
not for money
not for worldly goods
not for fame.

Too many times in this crazy world
we do things for all the wrong reasons.
But to write poetry
is to slumber in another place,
a freeing place.

To sign your name backwards
to sing off key
to trip upstairs
to eat desserts first
to drive on the wrong side of the road
to wear pajamas to work
to never brush your hair
to rhyme every sentence you utter
to paint mountains that are purple with suns that are green
to drink rain water off your tongue
to run on ice
to never wear sunscreen
to cook with an Easy Bake oven
to eat crayons and paste
to fly on the wings of a bug
to cry at the sight of spilled milk
to smell colors
to cook with paper and write with bananas
to hear the earth turn
to yell obscenities
to taste violets and marigolds and tulips
to jump in mud puddles.

Wendy Lewis

In Silence

I want to be bathed in silence
so that my spirit can rest easy.
I want to melt into the quiet
still and dark, alone and at peace.

Don't talk to me
unless it flows from you like a river.
Speak to me only as a child does,
no forcing, no holding back.[1]

Or hold my hand tightly,
and stand with me in the river
so that we both feel the tug
of the current with our feet.

In silence my spirit rises up
and I am one with the sky
and the earth and the trees.
The lichen-covered branches
are separate from me.
And in silence
I am grateful for that.

---

[1] Taken from "I Believe in All That Has Never Yet Been Spoken," by Rainer Maria Rilke.

Barbara Lazarony

Poetry is...

Poetry is...

A lady-bird beetle scampering through woodlands
wandering over rings in fallen logs
drinking from cups made of simple crushed maple leaves
almost unnoticeable, unless one
leans down, way down, and pauses.
And if one is fully aware and eager to "see,"
one may count the disappearance of each dot,
marking the passage of time.

Betsy Gilliland

Wishing

I make wishes a lot. Various people have taught me a variety of superstitions that encourage wishes. Scientific analysis may argue that my success rate has been less than stellar, but I live in a bubble of pure optimism, endlessly hoping that my wishes will come true.

My favorite method is wishing on loose eyelashes because I'm always losing them. When one comes out - I guess naturally is better than pulling, but either way works - I balance it on the tip of a finger, make my wish, and blow. If it flies away, the wish is supposed to come true. I get frustrated with my eyelashes when they stick to my fingertip and refuse to fly away; then I wonder if my wish will come true or not. Judging from how little romance I have found with the boys I've wished for on loose eyelashes, I think this is not such a successful technique.

Wishing on an evening's first star has a still lower success rate. Most of the time I wind up questioning my wish before I've even finished "Star light, star bright..." because I spot another star and wonder which was really out first. Sometimes I realize that my wishing star was a planet, a satellite, or even just an airplane.

The surprise of seeing a rare shooting star prevents me from wishing on them as well. Even one summer in Minnesota, lying on a dock during a meteor shower, each successive shooting star amazed me so much, I forgot to come up with an appropriate wish for the next one.

More terrestrially, I have always enjoyed making wishes on birthday candles. Even as a small child, I had a larger-than-average lung capacity and could blow all the candles out in one breath. I don't remember any of my childhood wishes. With a February birthday, I most likely forgot I had wished for something if I received it for Christmas ten months later.

I think most of my true wishes have been like that. If they came true, I had already forgotten I'd been wishing for them. If they didn't, I'd already forgotten that I'd made such a wish and thus was not overly disappointed.

I learned early on to make a wish when I found a penny on the ground. For a while I kept my avaricious gaze locked to the pavement, greedy for another opportunity at good luck. Since a college friend told me that only heads-up pennies brought wishes and those found tails-up actually caused bad luck, I've been less excited when I spy shiny copper lying on the sidewalk. I glance sideways at it in the hope that if I pretend I didn't really see it was heads-down, the tail will not take my wishes away.

This is not to say I no longer make wishes. On the contrary, whenever I lose an eyelash or walk outside at dusk, I make wishes. I'm content enough with my life, however, that I don't rely on the wishes for my happiness. I take each day as it comes and count any wishes that come true in stride with my other blessings. But it never hurts to make a wish.

Eileen McLaughlin

Writer's Block

To sit,
to stare,
to be nowhere.

The tick,
a tock,
drums the clock.

Draft,
scratch,
begin and again.

No thread
for words.
No source of urge.

Stymied,
silent
is the page.

Not heart
nor soul
lays bare this day.

The chimes ring "end."

The Authors

Betsy Gilliland

As a child, Betsy spent as much time at the Menlo Park library as most of her peers did on the soccer field. She yearned to visit the places she had read about, leaving her suburban California life far behind. By the time she returned from teaching English as a Peace Corps volunteer in Uzbekistan, Betsy had spent nearly three years living and traveling outside of the United States. She had stories to tell and no end of listeners within her circle of friends and family. She didn't start writing, however, until she began teaching composition to 18-year-olds at San Jose State University and realized that she should probably practice what she preached. Write On! helps her stay motivated every month.

Betsy published her first story, "Uzbekistan Party Power," in the Celebrations column of the *San Jose Mercury News*. Another story, "Meeting Mumina," won second prize in a contest sponsored by the *Glimpse Quarterly* and was published in the Glimpse Foundation's online magazine. Versions of both these stories were reprinted in a CD-ROM the Peace Corps created of stories written by returned volunteers from Central Asia. One of Betsy's long-term goals is to compile her stories into a book for armchair travelers who do not have the time to explore Central Asia in person.

Barbara Lazarony

Birth
Swimming
Reading
Candy striper
1st paying job
Outstanding of the Day
Flute
New school
Poetry assignment
Grandma & Grandpa died
Tim Thompson
New friends
David R. Lazarony Jr.
Graduation
College
Poetry class
Changing schools
Parents' Divorce
Florida
Married
House 1

Illness
Quitting job
California
House 2
PG House
Illness again
Depression
Poetry Circle
Reading
Gym
Meditation
Balance
Thyroid Cancer
Depression
Anxiety
OCD
Helping a friend
Reading
Quitting job
Journaling
Write On!

Wendy Lewis

Wendy Lewis never aspired to be a poet. Faced, however with divorce and cancer at mid-life, poetry became a healing consolation. She writes from a quiet peaceful place in her center, and never knows exactly what the words will say until they are on the page. It is a process of expressing her truest feelings, and there is a courageous vulnerability and self-acceptance in her voice. She is a member of John Fox's (author of *Poetic Medicine*) Carte Blanche poetry circle and recorded seven poems on a CD called, "Silence in the Sound of It," in November 2003.

Born Wendy Rappaport in Princeton, New Jersey, she holds a bachelors degree in Art and English from Douglass College, a division of Rutgers, The State University of New Jersey. She currently works in high-tech public relations in Silicon Valley.

Eileen McLaughlin

Without a doubt, the baggage of time, people and events is carried within Eileen. There lies a 1950s childhood and the pragmatic guidance of prohibition-formed parents. From there forward it was she who built: college, medical technology career, marriage, parenthood, community involvement, continuing education, divorce, and a high-tech marketing career. Then came the year 2000 and a nexus of timing and circumstance. Nine-to-five gave way and led to eco-volunteerism and activism, precinct walks, nonprofit education and the founding of Wildlife Stewards. All of this mixed with rejuvenation in Mexico, Crete, and Ireland, travel to various corners of the USA–and welcomed grandparenthood. Amidst it all, a persistent, nagging curiosity worked its way to the surface. Is there a writer in me? Thus came the day when she crossed a classroom threshold and first met some of the women who have become her Write On! peers.

Monique Mulbry

Monique Mulbry writes to "understand the ordinariness and extraordinariness of people, their relationships, and the worlds they inhabit." A Marketing Director at a high-tech firm in Silicon Valley, she leads a team of extremely talented visual artists and brand strategists in the craft of business communications. The stories and poem contained in *Facets and Fragments* are her first foray into published fiction.

Monique lives in Northern California with her husband, Matt, their two cats, Beamer and Miles, and their dog, Tucker.

Traci Post

Traci spends most of her time writing, driving and cooking. She believes that putting pen to paper, or fingers to keyboard, allows her to write and breathe her way through life's struggles and difficult times and capture the joys that fill us daily.

In addition to her poetry and short fiction, Traci has finished a contemporary romance novel and published the *Meals to Remember Family Cookbook* benefitting the Alzheimer's Association.

Traci lives in Almaden Valley with her husband, Dan, two inspiring teenage sons, Andrew and Clayton, and her devoted golden retriever, Jale.

Liza Wood

Long before she became an engineer, Liza wanted to be a writer. However, the concept of being a starving artist didn't appeal to her and she needed to explore life's adventures. During her journeys across Canada to California and back to Canada again, she has added many stories of life and love to her personal collection. Her favorite is how she met her husband at San Jose airport one fateful day in September 2001. Although she loves telling that story, she doesn't think it will make its way into her creative writing any time soon.

Over the years, writing has provided a creative balance in her hectic, logical life. Some day she hopes it will be more than that. Like the stories she contributed to this anthology, there will be an opportunity for a new beginning in her life. When it happens, she'll be ready to start the journey of being a novelist.

If you would like to contact the authors,
you can send an email to:
wewriteon@yahoo.com

For all other inquiries, please send mail to:

Write On!
PO Box 459
Los Gatos, CA 95031